THINKING
ABOUT
DEVIANCE

THE REYNOLDS SERIES IN SOCIOLOGY
Larry T. Reynolds, *Editor*
by **GENERAL HALL, INC.**

THINKING ABOUT DEVIANCE

PAUL HIGGINS

University of South Carolina

GENERAL HALL, INC.
Publishers
5 Talon Way
Dix Hills, New York 11746

Thinking About Deviance

GENERAL HALL, INC.
5 Talon Way
Dix Hills, New York 11746

Copyright © 1998 by General Hall, Inc.

Publisher: Ravi Mehra
Composition: *Graphics Division*, General Hall, Inc.

LIBRARY OF CONGRESS CATALOG CARD NUMBER: **98-73522**

ISBN: 1-882289-64-1 [paper]
      1-882289-65-X [cloth]

Manufactured in the United States of America

Contents

ACKNOWLEDGMENTS

Chuck Tucker and Larry Reynolds read rough drafts of this work and found merit in it. I appreciate their support. Patrick Saucier helped me obtain some of the published materials used in this work. Thanks Pat. I have benefitted in my own thinking about deviance from the wonderful work by many scholars. Citations to their works show my appreciation.

Leigh and our two daughters, Samantha and Cole, enrich my life each day. Part of that enrichment, which ultimately I would not wish away, is experiencing and thinking about deviance in our family.

INTRODUCTION

Think about the following:

• A town in the Northeast bans cursing, with a possible fine of $500 and up to three months in jail. Yet the police chief states that he has no intention of enforcing the ban (Banisky 1995).

• A government report shows that the percentage of young people ages twelve to seventeen who said they used illicit drugs in the month before being surveyed doubled from 1992 to 1995. These results become an issue in a recent presidential campaign (*The State* 1996f).

• A crew chief for an auto-racing team is fined thousands of dollars by the governing board of the racing sport for using "nonstandard" parts (*The State* 1996e).

• Neighborhood residents complain about a client of their state's mental health department, who has a history of violence, living in a community group home. Residents resent the number of community-care residents in their neighborhood (Berman 1994).

• Calling same-sex relations "perverse," the governor of Mississippi signs a law banning homosexual marriages in his state and denying recognition of homosexual marriages performed elsewhere (*The State* 1997b).

1

• A sheriff creates a temporary team of a dozen deputy sheriffs to enforce a county law regulating the loudness of music. The law sets a 62-decibel limit between 7 A.M. and 10 P.M. and a 55-decibel limit between 10 P.M. and 7 A.M., but leaves it to the sheriff's department to decide what is excessive (LeBlanc 1994a).

• A female employee of Israel's Ministry of Education returns to her car, which she had parked on the edge of an ultrareligious Jerusalem neighborhood. She finds the car's tires slashed and the car smeared with smashed eggs. A flyer taped nearby states that "parking in immodest dress" is forbidden. The employee had worn a short-sleeved dress cut above the knee with no stockings. Her attack is one of half-a-dozen recent attacks by ultra-Orthodox Jews, some of whom have also thrown garbage at motorists driving on The Sabbath (*The State* 1996d).

• In a small American town merchants and police develop and circulate a list of twenty-one suspected troublemakers who are informed that they will be arrested if they enter many of the downtown businesses. Every person on the list is black. Several of those listed sue city officials and merchants for violating their civil rights (*The State* 1995).

• Convicted rapists and other sex offenders in one state will be re-quired to pay to have a DNA sample preserved so that law en-forcement officers can compare those samples to evidence taken at crime scenes. This may help in crime investigations (Allard 1994).

• Officials in India begin to investigate the export of disabled children to wealthy Arab countries, where the children beg for a living. Their begging enriches their parents, who sell their chil-dren to traffickers, the traffickers, and the investors in this beg-ging scheme. Investors may have included schoolteachers, government workers, and local politicians (*The State* 1997a).

• A former president of a Dallas-based bank has paid $3,000 of $1 million in restitution ordered in a plea bargain that kept him out of prison for federal violations during the savings-and-loan scandals of the 1980s. He is not alone. The recovery rate for savings-and-loan scandal defendants involved in plea bargains is less than one penny on the dollar—.43 percent of $133.8 million in fines and restitutions, or $577,540 (Keil 1993).

• While more than 10,000 accusations of sexual abuse based on satanic rituals are found by researchers of a national agency involved with child abuse, no case is substantiated by investigators (Goleman 1994).

• A major tobacco company places full-page advertisements in newspapers complaining about government agencies and officials trying to prohibit smoking in America. The ad wonders if alcohol, caffeine, or high-fat foods (a picture of a hamburger is shown) will be targeted next (*The State* 1994b).

• A city board of education in the Rocky Mountains votes 4–3 to ban all nonacademic clubs at its three high schools. By doing so, a gay-straight alliance club at one of the high schools will be no more (*The State* 1996b).

Give the items that follow some thought:

• In the capital city of Cambodia, scores of police, ringing each school where thirteen- and fourteen-year-old students are taking highschool entrance exams, futilely try to stop cheating. Some, however, take bribes to help in the cheating. Children climb walls to pass notes to students taking the exams. Others yell through bullhorns into the classrooms. One student suffers a bloodied head when a rock with a crib sheet attached to it is thrown through his classroom's open window. Education officials consider discarding the test results but decide not to do so (*The State* 1996c).

• California and Arizona voters pass propositions that permit the use of illegal drugs, such as marijuana, if recommended by a doctor or prescribed by two doctors. While controversy continues about the medicinal value of marijuana for treating pain and other conditions, voters in these two states approve its use. Marijuana could even be used for treating migraine headaches. The director of the federal office on National Drug Control Policy, known as the nation's drug czar, "publicly warned doctors not to break federal law by prescribing marijuana" (Morganthau 1997, 20). If marijuana and other illicit drugs have medicinal value, they need to be tested rigorously and carefully controlled, as are other drugs, states the drug czar (McCaffrey 1997). The controversy will go to court.

- A Canadian husband is found not guilty of assaulting his wife. He claims that he was too drunk to know what he was doing. A Maryland man who shot and killed his wife several hours after unexpectedly returning home and finding her in bed with another man is reluctantly given an eighteen-month prison term by the presiding judge. The judge reluctantly sentences the offender to prison in order to uphold the integrity of the justice system, even though the judge feels that few married men would have the strength to walk away in a similar situation (*The State* 1994a and 1994c).

- "Hackers" may have stolen more than $2 billion worth of software over the Internet in a recent year (Meyer 1994).

- The Supreme Court in Israel rules that the national airline must grant the same-sex partner of a flight attendant the same benefits given to husbands and wives of heterosexual employees. Gay rights activists applaud the ruling (*The State* 1994d).

- Expert witnesses disagree about whether the deaths of two babies in a day-care center were due to natural causes or to violent shaking of the babies (LeBlanc 1994b). But the jury finds the operator of the day-care center guilty of murder, and the judge sentences the defendant to life in prison (Decker 1994).

- Federal safety investigators conduct a workplace-safety investigation at a poultry-processing plant after an employee who had been on the job one week is crushed to death in a cooling vat. The company had been cited for serious safety violations in the previous year (LeBlanc 1995).

• More than 650 former residents of "child-care homes" in North Wales make allegations of child abuse against 85 employees in 31 private or public facilities. Fifteen other investigations are being conducted elsewhere in Britain. Most who allege abuse are boys. Allegations include being raped, molested, force-fed dog food, pimped to prominent Britains, taken on sex trips abroad, and forced to act in pornographic films. The first complaints date to the 1960s, but they were not taken seriously. In the 1990s officials took new allegations more seriously, which has led to convictions and now to the widespread investigations (Chubbuck 1997).

• Without the knowledge of her parents, who are away at a wedding, a family's teenage daughter has several of her friends over to spend a weekend night. The daughter was to have spent the weekend with a friend. Other teens, not known to the daughter and her friends, learn of the unsupervised gathering, crash it, and vandalize the house through spray painting, cigarette burns, and razor slashes. The next-door neighbors, knowing that the parents are away for the weekend and understanding that the teenage daughter will be staying at a friend's house, see carloads of teens drive to the house but do not check. The parents refer to this incident when talking with the daughter about her future inappropriate behavior.

What do the above events have in common? They all concern *deviance*. Deviance fascinates many of us. We are intrigued by what seems to be the unusual, strange, even bizarre behavior of others. Some of us are "deviance junkies." We must have our daily "fix" of deviance—through the talk shows where people "tell all" or through the tabloid papers that "reveal all." Others of us merely "consume" deviance through the news, television programs, and the movies. Our fascination with deviance may enliven our spare time. But does that fascination enlighten us much?

Thinking about Deviance challenges you to wonder about deviance in ways that you likely have not considered before. It questions common sense about deviance. It may puzzle you. It may even trouble you. It may do so because to question what one knows to be obviously so may be discomforting. Some of the ideas I explore continue to discomfort me.

As you read and think about what follows, I hope that you will come to see the fundamental theme in this book: *We create deviance, all that it is.* This is an awesome responsibility, which we cannot escape, even if we try to do so. And I think that we do try to do so through much of our common sense about deviance. To state that we create deviance may not seem particularly profound or interesting. I hope that in the chapters to follow the statement's complexity and depth will be evident and its exploration will intrigue you. I return to the theme in the conclusion.

I urge you to try to take the thinking explored here as seriously as possible. While you may ultimately disagree with portions of what you read, try to see the line of reasoning that is presented. *Come to learn what you think about deviance and how you do so.* Careful reading, thoughtful consideration, then reasoned judgment, even if it ends in disagreement, will serve you best.

Thinking about Deviance also urges you to take your fascination with "their" deviance "over there," with the deviance of people and places seemingly far removed from you, and bring it closer to home, to your life and concerns. Most deviance, like the last item presented in the list, does not make the news. But your participation in the dramas of deviance is personally newsworthy and personally significant, as is that last item for me. *Thinking about Deviance* encourages you to think in nonobvious ways about your personal dramas of deviance. By doing so, you may develop new, more satisfying ways for participating in those dramas.

Thinking about Deviance does not try to provide all that one may wish to know. But it raises questions and offers new ways of making sense of those questions that you may not have thought about before. You decide whether turning what we often take for granted into serious, even disturbing, issues to explore helps you to think about deviance.

PROJECT

1. I began the introduction with summaries of many different instances of deviance in my local newspaper and other print media. In this project, you can explore the media—newspapers, magazines, television, movies, music, and so on. I have not yet defined deviance. But you can use your present understanding of deviance to help you identify stories, incidents, lyrics, and other items the media present that concern deviance. You might now do a little of this exploration. After reading chapter 1, you could redo your work using your new understanding of deviance. You could even make your exploration of media deviance more extensive. You might consider these projects after reading several of the early chapters. They are designed to provide you with a broader, less commonsensical view of deviance.

For example, examine a copy of your local newspaper and circle every item that you believe concerns deviance. Read the items that you have circled. Do not skip any section of the newspaper. You might do this for several days. What thoughts and/or questions come to mind after doing this project? How could you explore those questions?

You could do similar projects for other media. While watching various television programs, note incidents that involve deviance. Watch television news, record (with a brief phrase) all stories that are presented, and identify which stories concern deviance. Listen to various kinds of popular music and note which records/CDs concern deviance. Perhaps several people could listen to the top records/CDs for different kinds of music and compare the deviance presented in these different kinds. What insights and/or questions do you develop from these projects? How could you examine further your thoughts?

These projects could be made more complex if you wish. For example, you could introduce the element of time into the projects. You could compare newspapers of today and of past times concerning the presentation of deviance. You could record how many items of deviance are presented, where in the newspapers they are presented, the amount of space given to the items, and other characteristics of the presentations. Comparisons across time could also be made for records/CDs. What ideas do you generate from these comparisons? Or, you could ask several people to look at the same newspaper and identify the stories they felt concerned deviance. This would enable you to compare how people commonsensically think about deviance.

1

WHAT IS DEVIANCE?

When you think about deviance, what specific behaviors or conditions come to mind? Maybe you can list ten or so within two minutes. Please make your list before you continue reading.

Perhaps you thought of murder, child abuse, drug use, mental health difficulties, prostitution, pornography, and robbery. Maybe family violence, embezzlement, sexual fetishes, shoplifting, and corporate fraud came to mind. Did eating disorders such as anorexia nervosa or bulimia nervosa, suicide, mental retardation, burglary, homosexuality, and mugging occur to you? Did income tax cheating and academic cheating come to mind? Did you list still other items? Would you agree to include the items I presented?

More than 250 different instances came to mind when 180 people were surveyed several decades ago (Simmons 1965). I imagine that an equally diverse list would come to mind from a survey done today.

How are the items you listed deviant? How do you define deviance so that the items you listed fit the definition? Before continuing, please write your definition.

Those who are interested in a subject define it. Deviance is no exception. I believe that the most useful approach for thinking about deviance is this: *Deviance is behavior, thoughts, or attributes to which some people react negatively or would react negatively if they knew about it* (Goode 1994, chap. 2). I think this flexible definition enables us to include what we conventionally think of as deviant. It also points to other activities and conditions

9

that we might overlook but that may be usefully understood within the concept of deviance. Let's examine this approach. Compare your statement and reasoning with the statement and reasoning I and others use.

According to the approach I and others use, deviance can be *what people do, what they think, or even their characteristics.* If a teacher reprimands students for getting out of their seats, then the students have committed deviance. If a member of a club is shunned by other members after expressing particular opinions, then that member's thoughts are deviant. If acquaintances make fun of a person who is obese, then that person and the person's weight are deviant.

When behavior, thoughts, or attributes are *reacted to negatively*, they are deviant. The negative reactions may vary greatly. Execution, incarceration, banishment, and corporal punishment are harsh reactions. Less severe reactions might include expulsion, probation, fines, and demerits. Still less severe, though perhaps quite consequential, may be reprimands, ostracism, and belittling. Even urging or requiring individuals to seek treatment for their "problems" implies dissatisfaction with their problems. Whenever people react disapprovingly toward something, that something is deviant.

Behaviors, thoughts, or attributes can be deviant *even when no negative reaction has occurred.* No one may have reacted negatively because the behaviors, thoughts, or attributes were not known to those who would have reacted negatively. Much deviance is hidden. People sensibly hide what they know others will disapprove of. Their efforts to hide their actions, thoughts, or characteristics testify to the deviance of what they have hidden. If we know that people previously reacted negatively on similar occasions and would likely have done so if they knew about this occasion, then we can be reasonably confident that the behaviors, thoughts, or attributes are deviant.

Nevertheless, if people have followed the customs of their social group without realizing that their behavior is offensive to those from a different group or the society in which they now live *and* no one who may have been offended from the second group knows of the behavior, then that particular behavior at that time is *not* deviant. No negative reaction occurred, and no negative reaction was anticipated! If later, perhaps much later, people from the second group learn of the behavior and react negatively to it, then it has become deviant.

If people who acted according to their customs learn that the second group takes offense at their customary practices, are their actions deviant? When that happens and people from the first group anticipate negative reactions that could matter to their lives, then when they engage in their customary practices, they are engaging in deviance. Negative reactions, actual or anticipated, have come into play! That is the key.

Behaviors, thoughts, or attributes are deviant when *some people* react negatively or would do so if they knew about them. Many people may react negatively. Maybe just one person does. Many people, perhaps almost all, condemn strongly the "cold-blooded" killing of a person during a robbery, burglary, or sexual assault. The killer may be executed. Fewer people react so negatively to the abortion of a fetus. Those who act, think, or have characteristics to which others react negatively may or may not react negatively to themselves. They may feel ashamed. If they do, then their behavior, thoughts, or characteristics are deviant to them, too.

Through their negative reactions, people make behaviors, thoughts, and attributes deviant. How strongly people react negatively, how widespread their reactions are, and the power of those who react negatively are all important. If few people with little influence react mildly negatively, then their reactions may be insignificant. Those to whom their reactions are directed may not even be aware of the negative reactions. But if a government has passed laws banning certain behaviors, empowered officials to enforce those laws, and instituted harsh penalties for the violation of those laws, and if the citizens support those laws and their enforcement, then these reactions are much more consequential. Deviance varies as negative reactions vary.

Deviance speaks to that of which people disapprove. It is a flexible concept. It enables us to explore a wide variety of behaviors and conditions from the most widely condemned to the mildly rebuked. Certainly not all instances of deviance are equally significant, but all have in common the negative reactions of people. Certainly social scientists who explore deviance and officials who address deviance do not give equal attention to all that fits the definition of deviance offered here.

What is your evaluation of the definition offered here? How does it compare to yours? Does it make sense to you? Does it seem to be useful? Is it compatible with the ordinary use of the term? A standard dictionary states that deviance is that which significantly departs from what is considered acceptable or normal (Merriam-Webster 1986, 618).

Defining our interest is a start, not the end. Before we can explore issues about deviance that concern us, how can we decide what fits our definition? How can we decide what is deviant?

HOW CAN WE DECIDE WHAT IS DEVIANT?

How would you decide if some behavior, thought, or attribute is deviant? Remember that you are working with the definition offered here. After you have thought about this issue, then continue.

I think the surest way is to observe how people react to one another. If some people react negatively, then the focus of their reaction is deviant. If people hide something because they believe that others will react negatively to it, then what they have hidden is likely to be deviant. Observing people's reactions is the surest way to decide what is deviant, but it may be difficult to do so. You cannot observe people all the time and wherever they are. People may manipulate their reactions if you are observing them. Other difficulties can also occur.

What else could you do to decide what is deviant? You could ask people what is unacceptable to them. You could ask them to tell you what is wrong, bad, or offensive to them. Or you could ask them to tell you what they react negatively to. What do they punish? You could ask them to tell you what should be punished, even if they have not encountered that behavior, thought, or attribute. Perhaps to elicit their thoughts, you could give them lists of behaviors, thoughts, and attributes to evaluate as acceptable or not, deserving of some kind of negative reaction or not. All these and similar ways seek to document what people react to and evaluate negatively.

All these and similar ways also have shortcomings. Let me mention a few. Some people may not respond candidly. Some may not be fully aware of what they are taking offense at. Listing items of which people disapprove overlooks the complexity of social situations in which people do or do not respond negatively. People do not react to an action separate from the context within which it occurs. You might think about what some other limitations could be.

You could examine the standards people have established for themselves—their norms. For example, you could obtain their published, formally established, or publicly proclaimed laws, rules, and regulations that govern how people are to conduct themselves. What people publicly prohibit presumably is deviant. As I discuss shortly, however, looking to laws or rules may be misleading, too. Can you think of other ways to decide what is deviant? However you decide what is deviant, your focus should be on the negative reactions of people if you use the definition offered earlier.

WHAT DEVIANCE IS NOT

Deviance is that to which people react negatively. Nevertheless, many of us may have thought about deviance in other ways that we hope may be useful. These other approaches may be less useful than we first realize. These other ways of thinking about and defining deviance may unnecessarily narrow our view or mislead us. (See Goode 1994, chap. 2 as the basis for the following discussion.)

Some of us may think that certain behaviors by their very nature are unnatural, wrong, deviant. We may believe that killing, coercive sexual activity, beating children, homosexuality, and other acts or conditions are obviously and naturally wrong. We may believe that it does not matter whether or not people react negatively to these things; they are deviant. These acts and conditions are deviant because they violate the natural order of how life is supposed to be or they violate a divine decree, what a divine spirit has commanded life to be. Some acts will be deviant everywhere, anytime. This view, which many of us hold in varying ways, is *absolutist*.

An absolutist view is a powerful approach for *making* some behaviors deviant. When people use an absolutist view, then deviance is a profound transgression against nature or the divine. It is not simply something toward which some people, even the great majority of people in a society, express disapproval. An absolutist view can give strength to disapproving people's condemnation. It can also give horror to others' violations. Who would want to "burn in hell" or in other ways be forever banished from the divine for such absolute transgressions?

Nevertheless, an absolutist view overlooks the fundamental importance of people in deciding what is deviant. An absolutist view asserts that people are irrelevant to what is or is not deviant. According to an absolutist view, some behaviors are inherently wrong. Yet those who use an absolutist view cannot exclude people from the defining of deviance. After all, the absolutist view exists only through its establishment and use *by people*. People create their understandings of the divine or of nature. People decide which behaviors violate their understandings of the divine or of nature. People have done this at times very differently. In the name of their divinity, people have taken human life and have protested its taking.

As much as people might wish for the certainty that comes with an absolutist view, the certainty that some awesomely powerful, transcendent force has determined what should and should not be done, people must grapple with the issue of what to accept and what to condemn. They do grapple with that issue. Ironically, one way they do so is to develop and use an absolutist view in which they try to hide from themselves the awesome responsibility they have for deciding what is acceptable and unacceptable behavior.

An absolutist view overlooks the diversity of deviance. What people may react negatively to may vary greatly. Killing people has been acceptable. People have acceptably killed enemies, disobedient slaves, the seducers of wives, unwanted babies, and others.

Sex has often been coercive. Parents have routinely beaten children, even severely, throughout history and the world. And in other times and places what has been accepted has been condemned. *Stated rules* do not adequately tell us what is deviant. Statements of required, accepted, or prohibited behavior may often give good guidance as to how people will react. If people have made the effort, often great effort, to establish rules that prohibit specific behaviors, then we can tentatively assume they will likely react negatively to those prohibited behaviors. But abstract rules do not handle completely adequately the complexity of people interacting with one another in specific situations. Not all members of a group may support the rules. Members may support the rules to varying degrees. Those who do support the rules must apply them in specific, often complex situations. For example, my university prohibits conduct that "unnecessarily disturbs" others. That abstract rule must be applied in specific situations. What in the abstract may appear to be obviously deviant may in the specific situation not be so.

For example, much serious violence that seemingly violates rules prohibiting such behavior is often tolerated by American officials. When the offender and the victim are closely related, then assaults, even those resulting in severe bodily injury or death, often do not receive great attention. For example, when arrests are made, prosecutions and convictions may not occur. In Houston in 1969, 40 percent of people arrested for killing a relative were released without prosecution. Less than one-fourth of those arrested for killing a stranger were released without prosecution (Black 1983, 40). I take up this example from a different angle in a later chapter.

Instead of working from the abstract to the concrete, from the statement of a rule to its application in specific situations, it may be more useful to work from the specific to the abstract. How might we decide what are the rules group members use, if they use any rules at all? We may be able to decide by examining how people react to one another. By examining how people react to one another in diverse situations, we may be able to state more general patterns that fit our observations of their reactions. We may treat the general patterns as expressing the rules that the people are using, no matter what rules they have stated. To return to the example of Houston in 1969, a "rule" used by Houston officials was ("more or less"): Do not kill people, but particularly not strangers. Rules are crucial for giving people guidance as to what members of their community will and will not accept. But rules may not state adequately how people react to one another's behavior in specific situations.

Crime does not define deviance. Making behaviors illegal is a powerful way to express disapproval. But we may react negatively to behaviors without making the behaviors illegal. Consider the disapproval expressed within families, among friends, in organizations, in clubs, among neighbors, and in many other social groups that does not concern crime. For example, much deviance done by students is not illegal. Crime is an important segment of deviance, but only a part. Most deviance is not illegal.

Crime at times may not even be deviant. When people do not react negatively to what violates the law, then the apparent violations are not deviant, at least not to those who accepted what was done. Communities, including law enforcement agencies, often accept much violation of the law: violations of traffic, drug, alcohol, and prostitution laws, to mention a few.

Harm is not the test of deviance. What people react to negatively may or may not be harmful. What is harmful may or may not be deviant. Until recently, a well-known university in Texas did not permit university-sponsored dances. Is dancing harmful? How so? To whom? A twenty-year-old who drinks alcoholic beverages can be arrested for underage drinking. The establishment that sold the alcohol to the young person can be punished, too. Will one glass of beer harm that young adult? Homosexuality is strongly condemned by many people. What harm do consensual same-sex relations cause? As has been widely publicized, about 400,000 people in America die annually from smoking cigarettes. While many people now condemn smoking and governments have regulated where people can light up, smoking has been accepted, even promoted, in past times, even though many were concerned about its harm then. Tens of thousands of workers die annually due to workplace hazards and diseases. Governments typically do not react very punitively, however. Businesses may be fined as little as a few hundred or a few thousand dollars for workplace safety violations that contributed to the deaths of employees (Reiman 1995). *And people may genuinely disagree on what is and is not harmful.*

Many of us think of deviance as that which violates the *norms* of society. The dictionary from which I took a standard definition of deviance states that deviance is a "significant departure" from the "norms of a particular society." This is a useful way to think of deviance, but it is not completely satisfactory. Norms are the standards of acceptable and unacceptable conduct for a society or some group of people. The concerns that I raised for using rules or crime as a way to define deviance apply to norms, too. You may wish to review those limitations.

Certainly, people, groups, and societies develop standards of conduct for themselves and one another. Violations of those standards, those norms, can be followed by significant negative reactions. Knowing the norms of a group can be a promising start for understanding what is deviant within that group. But the norms may not be clear, agreed to by all, or easily applied. To know what the norms are and how they are used, one should look at how people react to one another. This brings us back to the definition of deviance offered earlier and to the most direct way for deciding what is deviant when one uses that definition: negative reactions.

CONCLUSION: CAN SOMETHING BE BOTH DEVIANT AND NOT DEVIANT?

To conclude this discussion, I raise a question: can something be deviant and not deviant? Please formulate your response, then continue.

An affirmative response doesn't seem possible. An object cannot be both something and not that something. Yet deviance is that to which some people react negatively. Therefore, to those who react negatively, the behavior, thought, or attribute is deviant. To those who do not react negatively, however, the behavior, thought, or attribute is not deviant. It may even be laudable. Therefore, something can be both deviant and not deviant simultaneously, though to different people. These reactions can even be nested within one another (Goode, 1994: 20). For example, the sale and use of illicit drugs remain widely disapproved of in America (Gallup 1996: 185–90). Only 14 percent of respondents favor or strongly favor legalizing all drugs. But 87 percent favor or strongly favor increasing funding for police to arrest local users and dealers, and 51 percent favor or strongly favor a mandatory death penalty for those convicted of smuggling large quantities of drugs into America. Local states and communities may be more tolerant of drug use, however, as witnessed by the propositions recently passed in Arizona and California allowing for the use of some drugs under particular circumstances, which I mentioned in the Introduction. And, of course, particular people may or may not respond negatively to drug use. A society can generally react negatively to particular behaviors, thoughts, or attributes, but particular audiences may not do so in specific situations (Goode 1994, 20).

You can imagine how differences in reactions can lead to serious conflict. And it does. Consider the conflict over abortion, cigarette smoking, drugs such as marijuana, drinking by those under twenty-one years of age, homosexuality, prostitution, and gambling. Americans disagree about accepting or condemning these actions and characteristics. People protest, sometimes violently so, for or against present policies and practices allowing or prohibiting these behaviors.

Everyday conflicts concerning what should or should not be deviant occur on a smaller, but still consequential, scale. Mothers and fathers may disagree with one another as to how their children should act. Teachers, school officials, and parents may disagree about how students should behave. Colleagues may respond differently to co-workers' actions. And some friends may accept while others condemn the same actions of a mutual friend. Think about the conflict of which you are aware concerning what is deviant within your social groups. Social life would be simpler if some behaviors were "just" deviant. But that is not so—and social life is not simple.

To conclude, let me return to the items you listed when you thought of specific behaviors and conditions that are deviant and to the possible instances of deviance I presented at the beginning of this discussion. Are your items or the ones I presented deviance? How would you know? Could they be both deviant and not deviant? What do you think?

PROJECTS

1. Now that we have explored how deviance can be defined, you could return to some of the projects suggested at the end of the introduction and retry them. For example, look again at the same newspapers to identify stories concerning deviance. Use this sociological approach that emphasizes negative reactions. Do you identify the same or different stories concerning deviance? Can you think of segments of your society that would not react negatively to what you take to be deviant in these stories? These or similar questions can be asked of other media that you could explore.

2. Ask people to mention as many items of deviance (items that they find wrong, bad, or unacceptable) that they can within a set time, say one minute. Compile the list. What items are mentioned frequently, which ones infrequently? What thoughts and/or questions come to mind? To extend this project, develop a list of items that were mentioned frequently and add to that list items that you think could be deviant to some people. Ask a sample of people to indicate which of those items on the list they find wrong, bad, or unacceptable. You might ask them to what degree they find the items wrong, bad or unacceptable. Do you think any particular segments of the population are more likely than other segments to find particular items deviant or not deviant? If so, record information about your respondents that will enable you to place them into one or another segment, such as different age categories or different levels of education. What does your project show?

3. Over the next day, several days, a week, or some set time, observe what people with whom you interact make deviant. To what do they react negatively? What do they criticize or judge to be wrong, bad, or unacceptable? If you notice one person making something deviant, then explore whether other people also make that deviant. For example, if one person criticizes people for their smoking, ask others with whom you interact if they, too, find smoking offensive. Do you notice if people are consistent about what they make deviant? For example, do they react negatively to a particular behavior whenever they witness it?

4. Apply the various possible ways deviance could be defined that were discussed in this chapter to a particular group or organization of which you are a member, such as a work group, club, or family. Would similar or different items be deviant depending on the various ways in which deviance is defined? For example, would the same items be deviant based on the primary definition of negative reactions as based on the possible definitions of harm, illegality, or formally stated norms? Put another way, are some behaviors legal within the social group on which you are focused but reacted to negatively? Does it matter, then, how those of us interested in deviance define our topic?

2

WHO IS DEVIANT?

When you think of *deviants*, who comes to mind? Please describe what images or people come to mind? When you are finished, then continue.

Textbook covers, like all kinds of packaging, present images to the consumers of what is inside. Let me describe as best as I can the covers of four textbooks on deviance. Perhaps the images or people that you described when thinking of deviants are similar to these textbook covers.

One cover presents the drawn head of a man imprisoned in a cage. Another presents a black and white photograph of the back of a man who appears to be sitting on a curb, across from some parked cars. The scene is somewhat hazy, almost foggy. A third presents a stylized picture in fuchsia pink of a man's elongated face that appears to be covered with a beard or ends in a jagged outline. I am not sure which it is. The distorted silhouette of a human figure, as if it is behind a translucent screen, adorns the cover of a fourth textbook. I return to these covers in a moment.

If you listed examples of people who are deviant, perhaps your list is similar to the following. Surely mass murderers and serial killers such as Jeffrey Dahmer, who not only killed more than a dozen people but also ate part of some of them, are deviant. Adolf Hitler and other ruthless dictators who exterminate their own citizens are deviant. Career offenders who rape, rob, and burglarize are deviant. Parents and others who burn children with cigarettes, stick their hands on hot stoves, strike them with electrical cords, or violently shake them are deviant. Homeless alcoholics are deviant. Those who hallucinate, hear imaginary voices, or experience other psychoses are deviant. Spouses who beat each other black and blue are deviant. Drug overlords who run international drug cartels are deviant. So, too, are the drug dealers who push drugs on young kids. So, too, is the crackhead. Police officers who take dirty money from drug dealers in order to let the dealers ply their trade are deviant. How about pornographers who make and sell smut, especially that involving children and youth? They're deviant. Gang bangers are deviant; prostitutes, too. Carjackers are obviously deviant, and so are many others. Let's return to those four textbook covers. What images of deviants do these four covers suggest to you? To me they suggest images that fit the list of those who are deviant that I presented above. The textbook covers and the list presented above indicate that those who are deviant are unusual, odd, weird, even bizarre people. They may even be "nuts, sluts, and preverts," as one sociologist remarked about the study of deviance (Liazos 1972, 103). If you noticed, the sociologist made a play on the spelling of the word "pervert" by changing it to "prevert." Those who are deviant are part of the fringe of society. But are they?

Who is deviant? My answer is that we all are. We all are deviant in diverse ways and to differing degrees. Deviance is everywhere. It is not confined to a fringe segment of society. Therefore, when we think about deviance, we can learn more about ourselves and our worlds, not just "those" people far removed from us.

Recall that deviance is behavior, thoughts, and attributes to which others take offense. Deviance is what others react to as unacceptable, bad, wrong, at times criminal, even immoral. People's negative reactions may run from mild disapproval to harsh condemnation and severe punishment. Deviance encompasses a wide range of behaviors and conditions, all unacceptable to some observers. Of course, widespread negative reactions or negative reactions by those with great resources are likely to be more consequential for a society or any particular group than a mild, idiosyncratic disapproval from a single person.

Don't we all act, think, or possess characteristics to which others at time take offense? Haven't we all experienced others taking offense toward us? Haven't all of us hidden some of our actions because we knew that others would condemn us? We are all deviant at times, though most of us are not deviant to the same extent as those with whom I began this discussion. But we may be more deviant, even more involved at times in what others would consider significant deviance, than many of us realize.

EVERYONE IS DEVIANT

Consider ordinary folks. Most of us are ordinary folks. Nothing wrong with that. Ordinary folks go to school, work, shop, pay their taxes and their bills, raise families, worship, enjoy leisure activities, belong to civic and other clubs, donate to charities, and much, much more. Ordinary folks are also deviant.

For example, ordinary folks commit crimes. Ninety-nine percent of the adults surveyed in New York City fifty years ago admitted to committing at least one of the forty-nine offenses listed on the survey. The average number of different *types* of offenses committed in adulthood was eleven for females and eighteen for males. For example, more than 80 percent of the men and women admitted to committing larceny; 26 percent of the men reported having stolen a car; over half of the men and 40 percent of the women admitted to committing tax evasion (Wallerstein and Wyle 1947). These were adults with no criminal record!

Twenty-five years later, adults in New Jersey, Iowa, and Oregon also admitted to committing illegal acts. Twenty-one percent reported stealing something worth $5 within the past five years, 32 percent gambled illegally within that time frame, 11 percent admitting assaulting another individual, and 12 percent admitted having cheated on their income taxes within the past five years (Tittle 1980, Chap. 2).

Tax cheating is so widespread that if all the money owed the federal government was collected, the federal budget would be balanced and even run a surplus. Between $150 billion and $400 billion are lost to the federal government from tax cheating each year. Approximately 6.5 million Americans do not even file their federal tax returns each year (Vartabedian 1996).

Many people will have been arrested by the time they are adults. The probabilities for arrest for a nontraffic offense over an American's life time is 60 percent for males and 16 percent for females (Gabor 1994: 53). Forty-seven percent of 1,000 boys born in Philadelphia in 1945 and followed until they were thirty years old had been arrested at least once (Gabor 1994: 56). One in every four males from a large American city is likely to be arrested for a serious violent or property crime, such as robbery, burglary, or assault. English males have an estimated 44 percent lifetime chance of being convicted for a nontraffic offense. Crime, often one form of serious deviance, is not confined to the fringes of society (Gabor, 1994, chap. 3).

Most young adults today have tried illicit drugs, though most are not regular users. For example, by their late twenties, more than 70 percent of American young adults have tried an illegal drug (Johnston, O'Malley, and Bachman 1996, 24). Yet, "only" 15 percent of young adults between the ages of nineteen and twenty-eight have used illegal drugs within the past thirty days, and less than 3 percent have smoked marijuana daily (Johnston, O'Malley, and Bachman 1996, 6).

Most youths have committed illegal acts (Empey 1978, 146). For example, two-thirds of a sample of Utah boys admitted to having been truant, 90 percent reported having stolen something worth less than $2, and two-thirds reported having destroyed property (Empey 1978, 146–48). Ninety-seven percent of male adolescents surveyed in Montreal, Canada, reported having committed at least one crime while an adolescent (Gabor 1994, 56).

Even the commission of illegal behavior among youths for one year may be higher than most of us realize. Twelve percent of youths aged eleven to seventeen in 1976 reported being involved in gang fights. Almost 50 percent hit other students. Eighteen percent had stolen something under $5. One-fourth had damaged family property; 16 percent had damaged school property; 18 percent had damaged other property. Thirty-two percent had been disorderly in public; 14 percent had been drunk in public. And 31 percent had been truant. All of this for just one year (Flanagan and Maguire 1990, 322)!

Many youths have tried illegal drugs and even more have drunk alcohol or smoked cigarettes. For example, by the end of the eighth grade, 35 percent of American students have tried an illicit drug (if inhalants are included), 43 percent of tenth-graders have done so, and 49 percent of twelfth-graders have done so. By the end of the eighth grade, 56 percent of students have tried alcohol, 71 percent of tenth-graders have drunk alcohol, and 80 percent of twelfth-graders have done so. Forty-six percent of eighth-graders have tried cigarettes, 57 percent of tenth-graders have done so, and 63 percent of twelfth graders have done so. Yet "only" 11 percent of eighth-graders have used illicit drugs in the past thirty days, 18 percent of tenth-graders have done so, and 22 percent of twelfth-graders have done so. Further, less than 1 percent of eighth-graders used marijuana daily, 2 percent of tenth-graders did so, and 3.6 percent of twelfth-graders did so. "Only" 1 percent of eighth-graders daily drank alcohol, 1.7 percent of tenth-graders, and 2.9 percent of twelfth-graders. Finally, 9 percent of eighth-graders smoked daily, 15 percent of tenth-graders did so, and 19 percent of twelfth-graders did so (though the percentages are cut approximately in half for daily use of half a pack or more) (Johnston, O'Malley, and Bachman 1996).

American workers routinely commit deviance against their employers. (As I explore in another chapter, employers also commit deviance against their employees.) For example, 29 percent of a sample of retail employees reported misusing the discount privilege, 27 percent of hospital employees admitted taking hospital supplies such as linens and bandages, and 14 percent of manufacturing employees reported taking raw materials from their companies, all of this done within the past year. More than half of the employees in each of those three sectors reported taking unauthorized long lunches or breaks within the past year (Hollinger and Clark 1983, chap. 3). Almost half of surveyed supermarket employees (44 percent) reported stealing from their supermarket (Arbetter 1994). Employee theft in the United States runs between $40 billion and $200 billion yearly (Gabor 1994, 73). Theft of time from employers, the "deliberate, premeditated stealing of paid time," not an idle chat, costs American employers an estimated $150 billion yearly (Gabor 1994, 75–76).

Almost half of more than 1,300 workers, managers, and executives recently surveyed admitted to committing in the past year unethical or illegal acts, such as cheating on an expense account, discriminating against co-workers, paying or accepting kickbacks, trading sex for sales, ignoring the violation of environmental laws, and secretly forging signatures (Jones 1997). Those surveyed were asked to report whether they had committed one or more of twenty-five listed unethical or illegal acts due to "pressure" of long hours, personal debt, job insecurity, sales quotas, and other pressures. Fifty-seven percent of respondents said that "they feel more pressure to be unethical than five years ago." Forty percent reported that the pressure to be unethical has worsened in the past year (Jones 1997, 2A).

Dishonesty, another form of deviance to many, is widespread. For example, 91 percent of Americans in a national survey reported lying regularly and 50 percent admitted to calling in sick when they were not (Gabor 1994, 64). More than fifty years ago, the honesty of garage, radio- and watch-repair employees was tested. Sixty-three percent of the garages, 64 percent of the radio-repair shops, and 40 percent of the watch-repair shops charged for unnecessary repairs (Gabor 1994, 59). Forty-nine percent of young people, ages eleven to seventeen, reported in 1976 that they had cheated on a school test in the past year; 64 percent of fifteen-year olds reported doing so (Flanagan and Maguire 1990, 323, 356). Two-thirds of thousands of high school students in nine schools in California and Wisconsin who were surveyed during the late 1980s and early 1990s reported that they had cheated on a test in the past year. Ninety percent reported that they had copied someone else's homework (Steinberg et al. 1996, 67). Forty percent of students polled at a Canadian university admitted to using the same paper in two or more classes, using an old exam to prepare for a test without the professor's permission, and/or plagiarizing within the past six months (Gabor 1994, 63–64).

Physical violence against family members is widespread. For example, more than 3 million couples kick, punch, stab, and/or commit other severe violence against one another each year. One and one-half million children under the age of seventeen are kicked, punched, bit, burned or scalded, or in other ways severely assaulted each year by their parents (Straus and Gelles 1988). Family violence is as American as apple pie.

Sexual violence occurs more than we may realize. More than one-fifth (22 percent) of women aged eighteen to fifty-nine contacted in a national survey reported that they had been "forced to do something sexual that they did not want to do by a man." Almost all of the men who forced these women to do something sexual were lovers, known well by the women, acquaintances, or spouses. Only 4 percent were strangers. In contrast, 2 percent of men reported being forced to do something sexual that they did not want to do (Michael et al. 1994, chap. 12).

Mental health problems are more prevalent than our commonsensical, stereotypical images of mental disorders may lead us to believe. We may think that it is only those who hear voices, think they are someone they are not, believe that creatures have invaded their bodies, and the like who have mental health problems. Not so. Many of us do. Almost half of Americans (48 percent) aged fifteen to fifty-four have experienced substance abuse/dependence and/or a mental disorder. Thirteen percent have experienced just drug or alcohol dependence or abuse, twenty-one percent have experienced just a mental disorder, and 14 percent have experienced both. Just in one recent year, 30 percent of Americans aged fifteen to fifty-four had experienced a substance abuse/disorder and/or a mental disorder. More than 5 million admissions to facilities specializing in mental health treatment occurred in 1990 (Rouse 1995, 37, 93).

Driving under the influence is not uncommon. Ten percent of Americans sixteen years and older who drove in the past year reported that they drove under the influence of alcohol or other drugs. Almost one-fifth (18 percent) of those between the ages of 16 and 34 reported having done so. One-fourth of men between twenty-one and thirty-four had done so (Rouse 1995, 19).

CONCLUSION

Who is deviant? Ordinary people are deviant. You, I, and other ordinary people are deviant in all realms of social life: the public arena, family and intimate relations, school, work, government, religion, sports, clubs and civic organizations, and elsewhere. I have presented some information to show how widespread is deviance.

Consider your actions. What deviance do you commit? In what realms do you commit deviance? What deviance have you committed in the past? What deviance are you engaged in now? Do you commit any deviance regularly, perhaps a couple of times a week, several times a month or each year, such as tax cheating? Perhaps you only very irregularly commit deviance. Keep in mind that deviance need not be horrific, pathological, dangerous, or even very serious. Much deviance is mundane, unexceptional, ordinary. For example, have you ever stolen from a store or your employer, drunk illegally, used illegal drugs, cheated, hit someone, cheated on your income taxes, cheated in school, violated requirements, or committed other routinely disapproved acts? Have others important to you, such as your parents, other family members, or friends, ever disapproved of the hours you kept, the way you talked or acted toward them, the effort you gave to some task, your attitude, or other actions, thoughts, or characteristics of yours? If so, then you were deviant.

I hope that you have not misunderstood me. I am not claiming that all of us are killers, rapists, burglars, abusers, and so on. All of us do commit deviance; most of us have committed illegal acts; an important percentage will be arrested; but relatively few of us commit many serious crimes. I am not saying that one form of deviance is equal to any other kind; that, for example, taking supplies from an employer for one's own use without authorization is equivalent to robbing a convenience store (though sometimes the amount of loss is greater in the former than the latter deviance).

Yet, when we think about deviance, we should not just have in mind some "fringe" segment of society. When we think about deviance, we can usefully think about ourselves, too.

PROJECTS

1. Create a list of deviant activities. Some may be criminal, some not. Some may relate to the sample of people who will respond to the list. For example, if students will constitute much of the sample, then include deviance such as academic cheating, cutting school, and other school deviance. Have people respond anonymously to the list. Ask them if they have ever committed the deviance and, if so, how much. You decide whether to leave that second question open ended or to provide a small number of possible alternatives, such as once, two or three times, four or more, and the like. Compile your results. For example, did anyone claim not to have committed any of the listed deviance? Which deviance was most committed?

2. Get some paperback textbooks on deviance. Examine the covers. What images come to mind? Ask people to examine the covers and report what images come to them. Do those images indicate that deviance focuses on what may be unusual, strange, exotic, bizarre? Do those images suggest that deviance is ordinary, routine, widely done by people?

3. This project may be difficult to do. Ask people to tell you whether they have committed deviance. If so, what deviance have they committed? Record their responses. Next, give them the definition of deviance presented in the first chapter. Ask them to think some more about the deviance they have committed. Ask them to add to their lists of deviance they have committed. Then, show them a fuller list of deviant activities, asking them to check what they have committed that they had not previously reported. Ask them whether they consider themselves deviant. For each person, compare the several responses (including the changing lists of deviance that was reported to have been committed). What sense do you make of these responses? For example, as you invite people to think more carefully about their deviance, do they recall (perhaps reinterpret) their having committed more deviance? Do people who have committed deviance, even "quite a bit" of deviance, state that they are not deviant? How do they explain that apparent inconsistency between their reported behavior and their self-characterization?

3

WHAT DO WE NEED TO KNOW TO UNDERSTAND DEVIANCE?

Deviance is that to which people react negatively or would do so if they knew about it. Employees' personal use of company computers, making lewd sexual remarks to a co-worker, underage drinking, performance-enhancing drug use by athletes, heretical beliefs, vandalism, mental illness, homosexuality, plagiarism by professors and students, running a red light, corporate fraud, lying, adultery, setting off fire alarms in a school, being greatly overweight, talking back to a person in authority, shakedown of drug dealers by law enforcement officers, having alcoholic problems, unauthorized release of hazardous waste, and much, much more may be deviant.

Much may be deviant. But to understand deviance, what do we need to know? What should we explore in order to develop an adequate grasp of deviance? Please think about this question, formulate your response, then continue.

If you had difficulty deciding what we need to explore in order to understand deviance, don't worry. It is difficult to know what we need to know about any issue, and certainly about deviance.

Perhaps you listed that we need to know what is accepted and what is not in society. Maybe you wondered about different societies' views of deviance. Did you list child abuse, crime, mental illness, and other likely kinds of deviance that we need to explore in order to understand deviance? I imagine that you and many other readers listed that we need to investigate why people commit deviance. What causes people to commit deviance? may be the major question that many believe we need to address to

31

understand deviance. Certainly it is an important issue for understanding deviance. But that is not all we need to know about
deviance.
     We will enhance greatly our understanding if we enlarge our
focus when thinking about deviance. Instead of solely (or even
primarily) focusing on the people who commit deviance—on
what causes them to act unacceptably—we might profitably explore how the rest of us participate in the dramas of deviance.
Deviance is produced through the actions of all of us as we
manage the challenges of living and acting together. I think it
may be useful to consider the following processes (or actions that
address particular challenges) through which we produce those
dramas of deviance (Higgins and Butler 1982, chap. 1).

PROCESSES PRODUCING DEVIANCE

First, *how do people produce their understanding about deviance*? How do they know that they have produced knowledge,
not nonsense? At one time, people thought that biological abnormalities of people forced them to commit crime. Criminals were
thought to be atavists, a "throwback" to an earlier form of human.
Today we take that knowledge as nonsense (Gould 1981, 123–
43), though the biologies of people do matter in deviance. Or,
throughout this century, the interest in and acceptance of "broken
homes" as a key cause of juvenile delinquency has waxed and
waned (Wilkerson 1974). Nowadays, some social scientists have
concluded that it is not as important as many might imagine
(Wilson and Herrnstein 1985, chap. 9). Others continue to believe
that a broken home does promote illegal behavior (Smith and Jarjoura 1988). How did that interest wax and wane, and why have
some now concluded that broken families are not as important as
many imagine?
     One specific issue within the challenge of producing under-
standing about deviance is to decide how much deviance exists.
How much crime, school misconduct, mental health problems,
academic cheating, sexual harassment, and other kinds of deviance exist? When a newspaper reports that so much crime has

occurred locally in the past year or that crime rates have increased or decreased, how should we evaluate that information? Deviance comes to exist for us, to have its shape and characteristics, through what we know about it.

Second, *how is it that something is deviant*? How is it that some kinds of killing, making lewd sexual remarks to a colleague, drinking if under the age of twenty-one, dumping toxic wastes into a stream, homosexuality, belief in witches, and other acts, thoughts, and/or conditions are deviant (if indeed they are deviant among a particular people at a particular time)? Perhaps it seems obvious to you. Some actions or characteristics are just deviant. But recall my earlier discussion of the shortcomings of an absolute view. Deviance is not absolute, even if we may wish that it were. And with additional thought, you realize that what is deviant today in our society was not necessarily deviant in past times, and vice versa. None of the behaviors and conditions mentioned above have always been deviant. Therefore, how do people come to make some acts and characteristics deviant but not others?

Certainly, we would want to know *what causes people to commit deviance*. Why do people use illegal drugs, assault, cheat, commit fraud, and so much more? Why have you committed deviance? I believe social scientists and citizens have been most interested in this question. Many explanations have been developed. If we understand why people commit deviance, goes the reasoning, then we may be more able to reduce or prevent it.

Next, *how do those who commit deviance do it*? How do people who drink underage, cheat academically, mug, murder, hack computers, commit corporate fraud, and commit other deviance "pull off" their deviance? What do they do to accomplish their deviant acts? Knowing what causes people to commit deviance does not tell us how they do it.

Law enforcement officers, mental health professionals, social workers, schoolteachers and administrators, and many other officials try to spot deviance and notice or uncover those who commit it. Officials must do so in order to handle the matter. Police officers patrol their beats, mental health professionals examine those who appear before them, social workers investigate cases of suspected abuse, schoolteachers and administrators look out for drug use and other deviance in their schools. How do these officials observe deviance? What procedures do they use? What challenges do they confront in trying to observe deviance? But is it just officials who encounter the challenge of spotting deviance? Or might family members, friends, co-workers, dorm mates, and many others also experience that challenge? *How do people recognize deviance?*

Once law enforcement officers, mental health professionals, social workers, schoolteachers and administrators, other officials, and everyday citizens have spotted deviance, they confront a difficult question: What kind of person is the individual who did the deviance? What is the person's true identity? For example, juries that sit on capital punishment cases must decide whether to sentence those found guilty of murder to death or to life in prison. Their decision partly rests on what kind of person the convicted murderer is. Teachers and school administrators decide whether the student who misbehaves is basically a "good" kid or not. Knowing that someone has done deviance does not tell us what kind of person that offender is. *How do officials and others decide the identity of those who commit deviance?*

I believe that most people are concerned to learn why people commit deviance in order to do something about it. *How do officials and ordinary citizens deal with deviance?* What do they do, why, and with what consequences? What could they do instead?

Those who are deviant are not passive bystanders in this drama of deviance. They manage their deviant status as they try to meet their concerns. They may hide or cover their deviance; participate with similar others in voluntary organizations or communities, such as gay communities; or try to become conventional through changing their behavior or changing the reactions of others. *How do those who are deviant cope with conventional society and with what consequences?*

We need to know about all the questions I have just mentioned: How do people produce their understanding of deviance? How do people make some actions or characteristics deviant and not others? What causes people to commit deviance? How do people "pull off" deviance? How do officials and others recognize deviance? How do they decide the identities of those who commit deviance? How do they deal with deviance? How do those who are deviant cope with conventional society? People create the dramas of deviance as they confront and handle these eight challenges. They also create the dramas of any particular kind of deviance, such as sexual harassment, corporate fraud, and academic cheating, as they manage those eight challenges. We need to know much more about deviance than why people commit it.

In the chapters that follow, I explore various issues that can be placed within these eight processes. Some discussions are nonobvious; others may be very disturbing. I hope that all are intriguing. However, I do not nor could I examine all that we might need to know about deviance. We have not created all that we need to know. We never will because thinking about deviance is a never-ending challenge. Instead, the chapters are intended to invite you and to excite you to think about deviance in ways that you had not done before.

HOW DO YOU PARTICIPATE IN DEVIANCE?

Now, how do you participate in the dramas of deviance? Please take some time to list specific ways in which you have participated in these eight processes that make up the phenomenon of deviance. When you finish, then continue.

When I ask my students to list anonymously how they participate or have participated in the dramas of deviance, they provide a wide variety of ways. They have mentioned smoking; lending out their IDs; using illegal drugs; driving recklessly; cheating on tests and on taxes; being bisexual; assaulting others; cursing; drinking heavily; stealing a birthday present at a party; stealing computer programs; telling a cashier that water, not a clear soft drink, was in the glass; and many other items.

These young people have participated in the dramas of deviance in diverse ways. But do you notice anything else about the list? Look at it again before you continue.

I notice that the young people I asked to list how they participated in the dramas of deviance have misunderstood the question. They have not yet expanded their view in thinking about deviance. Instead, their focus is solely or primarily on committing deviant behavior. They have listed deviance they have committed. Perhaps you, too, solely or primarily focused on the deviance you have done. If so, then you might review the eight challenges that I explored and list once again the ways in which you have participated or at present do participate in the dramas of deviance.

We all help to produce the dramas of deviance, perhaps much more than we realize. Consider each of the eight challenges. First, through reading, listening to others, classes we take, and our own experiences, we develop understanding about deviance. For example, we develop understanding about why people commit deviance or how best to "pull off" underage drinking or other deviance. We may read about the warning signs of alcohol or mental health problems. We may learn from others how to handle people who have committed deviance. We also develop understanding about how much deviance exists. We may even participate in the production of those statistics. For example, when you report or do not report to the police that your book bag has been taken or that someone attempted to assault you, you have helped to create how much deviance is recorded. You and I, in diverse ways, create understandings of deviance.

Next, how do you participate in making some things deviant and not others? I imagine that you vote in political contests for candidates who legislate what is acceptable behavior. You may even help in political campaigns to elect politicians. Perhaps you vote in referendums where you and other citizens pass or defeat legislation that shapes what is acceptable or unacceptable in your jurisdiction. But consider the everyday worlds in which you live. Do you help to make, change, or oppose standards for behavior in your family, among friends, in clubs and organizations of which you are a member? Do you support, tolerate, or don't think much about present standards, not challenging them? For example, are you involved in dramas about acceptable attire, language, sexual behavior, drinking, obligations to one's group, and so on?

Now, what caused or causes you to commit deviance? All of us have committed deviance. How would you explain your deviance? Yet, how we understand our commission of deviance may not be adequate to social scientists who explore this question.

While social scientists may be interested in learning how people understand their own deviance, social scientists may not accept people's explanations as their scientific explanations. Are the social scientists being arrogant, simply dismissing the explanations provided by those who commit deviance? Perhaps the social scientists realize that all people act without necessarily understanding well how they come to act as they do.

When you committed deviance, how did you "pull it off"? For example, if you are underage and have drunk alcohol at a bar or elsewhere, which is common among many young adults, certainly among the young adults I teach, how did you do it? How did you obtain fake identification, prepare your appearance, create your confidence, select the bar and even the time and date, present yourself at the bar, and so on? Even pulling off what many would consider to be a very mild form of deviance, underage drinking, may take much more work than we first imagine.

Have you ever become suspicious of a family member, friend, colleague, or someone else committing deviance? Perhaps you became suspicious of someone using illegal drugs, having an alcohol problem, stealing, and so on? How did you become suspicious? What did you do after becoming suspicious? Did you conclude that the person committed deviance or not? Perhaps you work as a sales associate in a store or as an employee in other businesses where you have organizational responsibility for noticing deviance. What training did you receive to spot deviance? What procedures do you use? Have you ever noticed someone shoplifting or committing other deviance at your place of work? Have you had the challenge of recognizing your own deviance? Perhaps you drank, dieted, or acted in other ways that became a "problem," but it took you some time to realize that your actions had become deviant. Many of us experience that challenge.

If you did conclude that someone committed deviance, then what kind of person was the individual? Was the person who cheated, stole, did drugs, or committed some other deviance a basically good person or not? How did you decide who the person was "really"?

I imagine that you have dealt with deviance in diverse situations and ways. As a family member, friend, organizational member, colleague, and in other ways you have handled deviance. Have you ignored it, warned or tried to talk with the offender, tried to get help for the offender, retaliated, reported it to officials, and so on? Perhaps you dealt with it formally as an officer in a club or organization? Maybe you have volunteered in treatment programs or programs that try to prevent people from becoming deviant, such as youth programs? We all deal with deviance.

As someone who has committed deviance, how have you tried to cope with conventional society? Have you tried to counter others' accusations about your deviance by vehemently denying that you were involved or by justifying what you did? Have you tried to hide your deviance, passing as if you were conventional? For example, coming home drunk, perhaps you tried to give your parents the impression that you were very tired. Did you participate with others who were similarly deviant, drawing support from them to cope with what you and fellow deviants saw as the cruelties of conventional society? Perhaps you simply gave up the deviance, returning to a conventional way of life. Have you participated in any self-help groups? Having committed deviance, all of us do cope with conventional society.

You may have been involved in the dramas of deviance in several ways for any specific episode. For example, you may have eventually discovered that a friend was doing drugs; concluded that the friend was experiencing painful relations with family members, thus, still a good person; and helped the friend get some treatment for the drug problems and family difficulties. You noticed deviance, identified what kind of person your friend was, and dealt with the deviance. Your and my participation in deviance may be quite complex. I urge you to be aware of all the ways in which you participate in the dramas of deviance.

CONCLUSION

Deviance is more complex than we typically imagine. Most people are curious about why people commit all kinds of deviance, particularly deviance that is heinous, bizarre, or other than what they themselves commit. But why people commit deviance is only one important issue. Instead, through many interrelated processes, people produce deviance. Now, what do you think needs to be explored in order to understand deviance adequately?

PROJECTS

1. Explore how you participate in the phenomenon of deviance. How do you produce your understandings of deviance? Do you rely on the mass media, textbooks, experts, family or friends, or common sense? Do you check for yourself what you think you know about deviance? How do you help to contribute to the statistics about deviance? For example, do you report instances of deviance to appropriate officials? Second, how have you participated in making what is deviant within your group or community? Have you accepted, rejected, proposed, voted for, supported, and/or in other ways tried to have your group or community establish some action as offensive or resisted that being done? Third, what do you think has caused you to commit the deviance you have done? How would you explain that?

Fourth, when you committed deviance, how did you pull it off? How did you pull off underage drinking, cheating on a test, shoplifting or some other deviance that you committed? Examine carefully what you did to commit that deviance. You may be surprised how much work goes into committing even the "simplest" deviance. Fifth, when and how did you come to recognize that a family member, friend, colleague, or other person in your social world was involved in deviance? Or did you suspect that someone you know was involved in deviance but later came to decide that the person was not? How did that occur?

Sixth, when you decided that someone was involved in deviance, what kind of person did you think the offender was? Did you "know" the offender to be still quite conventional, or did you "realize" that the offender was quite deviant? Did others see the offender as you did or differently? Next, how have you dealt with family members, friends, colleagues, or other people who

committed deviance? Did you warn, counsel, punish, urge treatment, or in other ways deal with the offender? Did you try a variety of strategies, one after the other, if previous approaches
were not successful? If you did, when did you call officials to
take care of the deviance?

Finally, how have you as a deviant coped with conventional
society? Did you try to deny your deviance and assert your inno-
cence/conventionality? Did you try to account for your deviance,
lessening your responsibility or the seriousness of the deviance?
Did you join others involved in the deviance as a means of
avoiding those who would be offended by you and as a way of
developing a set of beliefs and a social circle to shield you from
others' negative reactions? Did you try to change your deviance,
perhaps through participation in a self-help group or through
giving up the deviance? Did you try to present yourself to others
as conventional, passing as someone who was not doing drugs,
had not cheated on a test, and so on? Did you challenge the deviant status of what you did or your characteristics? For example,
did you challenge the standards of your group that makes a particular behavior unacceptable, trying to get your group to revise
what it makes deviant? How have you been involved in the complex phenomenon of deviance?

2. The above project could explore how friends or others you
know are involved in the phenomenon of deviance. This could be
sensitive. Certainly, some of the processes that make up the phenomenon of deviance, such as what causes a person to do deviance, may be more sensitive for a friend to discuss that some of
the other processes.

3. Or, explore media stories of deviance, for example those
in newspapers, to see which processes of deviance are more
likely to be presented. I imagine that you will find some of the
processes are much more likely to be presented than are others. If
so, how would you explain that?

4

IS DEVIANCE A WART ON, OR THE WOOF, OF SOCIAL LIFE?

Beating people,, tattling, taking without permission, corporate fraud, failure to report one's income fully, illegal drug use, unauthorized entry into a house to steal some of its contents, imagining that dead presidents are speaking to you, selling repaired merchandise as if it were new, nudity in a park, chronic tardiness for work, and much more are often deviant. Deviance is unwelcomed, even resisted, by those who find it offensive. That seems obvious. Now, let's think nonobviously about deviance.

Let's explore the place of deviance in society. To do so, please react to the following two metaphors. Explain what you take those metaphors to mean. Do you think either is useful for depicting the place of deviance in social life? If so, then how so? If not, then why not? You may wish to take some time to respond to these two metaphors. I don't believe their possible meanings leap out at us. After you have grappled with these two metaphors, then continue.

The first metaphor is this: *Deviance is an unsightly wart, perhaps even a cancerous growth, on the body of social life.* The second metaphor is this: *Deviance is the woof of the fabric of social life.* (*Woof* is the thread or yarn woven across the warp. The warp is the yarn placed lengthwise in a loom.) Use the questions mentioned above to guide you in thinking about these metaphors and in writing your response.

What do you take the two metaphors to mean? I take the first one—deviance is an unsightly wart on the body of social life—to mean that deviance spoils social life. It blemishes, perhaps

41

damages, even mortally harms social life. Without deviance, social life would be more beautiful, even healthier.

What did you make of the second metaphor: deviance is the woof of the fabric of social life? It is an odd one; perhaps obscure too. I wrote it to mean that deviance is an essential feature of social life. Through deviance, social life is created. Just as a woven fabric cannot exist without the woof interwoven across the warp, social life cannot exist without deviance. Did you develop some other ideas out of these metaphors? If so, that is fine. Metaphors are meant to be suggestive, not definitive.

Do you think these metaphors are useful for depicting deviance, for enabling us to begin to think fundamentally about deviance? I think they are. Yet the two metaphors provide starkly contrasting images of deviance. I believe the second metaphor is nonobvious. I believe it is also more useful for us in thinking about deviance. You decide as you continue reading.

DEVIANCE AS UNWANTED, UNNATURAL PATHOLOGY

The first metaphor provides a commonsensical view of deviance. It indicates that deviance detracts from, or is pathological to, social life. Without deviance, social life would not be flawed, perhaps fatally flawed. Let me build upon this imagery.

Many of us take social life for granted. We may not think deeply about it. We live it, not analyze it, as my older daughter tells me. We may assume that people naturally live and act together. Something inside them— perhaps their evolutionary development as encapsulated in their genes—or something outside them—perhaps divine will—makes that so. We realize that people do not always "get along," but we may assume that they are "meant" to do so. If it were not for biological flaws, deviations from a divinely prescribed path, or some other aberrations that are not part of the essence of humans and of social life, people would live and act together successfully, according to this assumption held by many of us. If we could excise that wart of deviance or remove or put into remission that cancerous deviance, then social life would be wholesome, as it is meant to be. Deviance is a pathogen that damages the normal, healthy functioning of society, according to this first metaphor.

Certainly this metaphor presents some truth about deviance. Through deviance, people at times create great harm to and heartache for one another. Deviance can be horrifyingly destructive. Yet I think this first metaphor does not encourage us to think more critically in nonobvious ways about deviance. The first metaphor may suggest images of social life that blind us to the challenges of living and acting together.

DEVIANCE AS AN ESSENTIAL COMPONENT OF SOCIAL LIFE

I find the second metaphor more useful than the first. In being the woof of the fabric of social life, deviance is essential for social life. Without the woof, the fabric does not exist. Without deviance, social life does not exist. We certainly may abhor the destruction caused by some deviance, but deviance is fundamental to human life. Let me explore how that is so.

Social life is a never-ending challenge. Nothing dictates how people will act with one another. Nothing guarantees that they will live and act together adequately. Evolution has led humans to be social animals; people become fully human with others. Our nature as a species provides capacities, biological needs, and predispositions. It does not dictate how people will act within those capacities, needs, and predispositions. Each moment people create their lives; each moment they produce social life. The next moment waits to be made by people. It is not predetermined (Higgins 1994; Stewart, forthcoming).

Humans have a great capacity to act in many ways. At any moment they could exercise any of those capacities. They could run, jump, move one way or another, sit, talk softly or loudly, strike, caress, think, laugh, and on and on. Yet they do not have unlimited capacity. They cannot flap their arms and fly like an eagle. They cannot live for several hundred years, as some trees do.

Humans have biological needs that must be satisfied if they are to survive. Humans must nourish their body, maintain vital functioning, procreate. Those needs do not dictate what humans will do. Those needs do not force humans to meet the needs. People do fast for long periods of time, even to death. People may be celibate for their entire lives.

Humans have genetic, hormonal, and other predispositions. Scholars continue to investigate what those are. For example, it appears that males are biologically predisposed to be more aggressive than females are. Most people are predisposed to be sexually aroused by those of the other sex. But these predispositions do not compel people to act in any particular way at any moment (Gould 1978; Harris 1989). Human social life is made moment by moment by people.

People produce their lives and social life as they seek to meet their goals. I take up this point in greater detail in chapter 9. Nothing dictates toward what goals people will strive. People create those goals.

People also create whatever meaning their lives and social life have for them. People decide what is worthy, honorable, beautiful, horrific, and so on. Humans create the values, dreams, principles, and images that at times guide their efforts.

Consider a simple example. Consider art. When some of us view a particular piece of art, or even much art, it is very worthy to us. We experience it to be intriguing, bold, exciting, thought provoking, pleasing, and so on. Others see it to be boring, ugly, puzzling, a waste of time. But the art is not any of that in and of itself. It becomes whatever meaning we have made for it. So it is for all of our world (Higgins 1994, chap. 3).

Therefore, humans continually face the awesome challenges of trying to live and act together, figuring out ways to do so, and in the process giving meaning to themselves and their world. They face these challenges when nothing dictates what to do, what meaning to give. They face the challenges when they have only themselves on whom to depend.

I imagine that some readers have become very upset. Some may take these words to mean that I am dismissing divine will and guidance. I am not. Instead, people *together* make powerfully, unquestioningly alive for themselves the divine will and guidance they strive to follow and take comfort in. That, too, is a challenge. Different people address that challenge in differing ways. Religions have varied greatly throughout human existence and do so today.

Where, then, is the place of deviance in these never-ending challenges faced by humans? *It is central to the challenges.* People produce deviance as they try to meet the challenges of living and acting together and of giving meaning to their existence. Deviance would not exist if there were no challenges. But if there were no challenges, then human existence would be fundamentally different from what it now is. Deviance is a powerful means through which people try to confront the primary challenges of human existence.

Consider: In the struggle to give meaning to life, people create understandings and feelings of what is honorable or not, of what is worthy or not, of what is acceptable or not. Those understandings become crucial components of what it is to be human. In creating those understandings, people are simultaneously creating what is deviant and the possibility for deviance to occur. The worthy is known in part by its contrast to the unworthy. The conventional and acceptable are known in contrast to the deviant. Behavior that is part of human capacity has now become deviant. People can use that deviant status as a means to try to "get" one another to act in certain ways and not in other ways. It is a powerful means for narrowing how people act out of the enormous range of how they could act. "Don't do that because it is wrong, immoral, illegal, unacceptable, unnatural, and so on." People can also apply that deviant status to acts they contemplate as they decide what to do next. Deviance, then, is a crucial component in people's struggle to live and act together, to make known to themselves how to act, to make themselves who they are.

For example, by creating some forms of sexual behavior as virtuous, people create other forms as deviant, and vice versa. Thus the deviance of what we nowadays call sexual assault may become a powerful way to proclaim how people are at present expected to live and act together. Recall, humans have a great capacity to act in a wide variety of ways. Nothing forces them to act in any particular way. Through regulations, punishment, moral condemnation, and much more, the deviance of sexual assault becomes a means to try to get people to live and act in specific ways. Of course, no means is completely successful.

By making deviant some forms of sexual behavior, people are also shaping who they are as persons. They are giving meaning to their identities. They have become persons in which the boundaries of their sexuality are drawn in certain ways and not others. Even to consider engaging in those now-deviant sexual behaviors is to confront their identities as normal, ordinary people.

Even if the negative reactions, the hallmark of deviance, were completely successful in getting people to act in appropriate ways, people would not have gotten rid of deviance. It would still be a crucial component of social life. Yes, people might not be committing *that* deviant behavior, for which many may be pleased, but deviance would still exist. The essence of deviance is the negative reactions—actual and potential negative reactions. Even without deviant behavior, deviance would still be central to the challenge of social life. It would be through deviance— through actual and potential negative reactions—and much more (such as bonds of trust among people) that deviant behavior did not occur, that people acted in particular, acceptable ways. But they knew what was acceptable by making deviant some potential behavior. The success in this case of making something deviant shows that deviance is a crucial component of social life.

The same holds for every instance or kind of deviance. Through making some killing, some business transactions, some traffic behavior, some governmental action, some drug use, some mental functioning, some appearance, and on and on deviant, people are trying to figure out how to live and act together and to give meaning to their lives. Deviance is a crucial component in meeting those challenges of human existence.

Deviance is a crucial component in confronting the challenges of social life in another, yet related, way. As I noted above and as I explore in a later chapter, people direct themselves to meet their goals. But their goals may not be others' goals. The goals of different people may clash. Deviance can be crucial to this conflict of goals. People can and do use deviance—both reacting negatively to some things and doing those things to which others react negatively—to try to meet their goals. Consider some businesspeople and the public. The public, or segments of it, may wish to have clean air and water. The businesspeople may desire to make their products with as little cost as possible. The public may also wish to be employed and to have products to buy. The businesspeople, too, may be concerned about their environment. Let's not put anyone in a white or black hat. To produce their products at a low cost, the businesspeople may discharge waste into the environment. Perhaps certain kinds of discharge will become reacted to as deviant. The public, or segments of it, may protest, even violently, against businesspeople. Perhaps certain forms of protest will be deviant. But whatever the scenario, which can become very complex, the businesspeople and the public can use deviance—both negative reactions to others' unwanted behavior as well as their own unacceptable behavior—to further their concerns. Deviance is integral to human existence.

CONCLUSION

What do you think? Is deviance to be wished away, or is it an integral, essential feature of social life? Is it a wart or a more serious malignant growth affecting the otherwise healthy social body? Or, in nonobvious ways, is it the woof of social life? We certainly may wish to be rid of the harm and the heartache of some deviance. But deviance—the making unacceptable of some of human existence, of some human action, thought, and attributes—is crucial to human existence. Deviance is one of the fundamental means by which humans live and act together. It is within social frameworks of what people make deviant or acceptable that people become who they are!

Can you apply this argument to your more personal worlds: family, friendship groups, clubs, organizations, work, and so on? Are living and acting together and giving meaning to one's existence never-ending challenges in those social worlds? Do you and the other participants use deviance in confronting those challenges, in telling one another how to be in those worlds, who to be in those worlds?

For example, females in my classes who are in sororities have often written of how their sorority makes deviant such acts as "low" grades, smoking, underage drinking, missing meetings, not paying one's dues, not participating in civic projects, and so on. The "respectable" sorority sister does not do such things, *is not such a person!*

Is deviance important in your worlds as people pursue their concerns, concerns that may conflict with other participants' concerns? Consider the conflicts between parents and their teenage children. The parents may react negatively to some of their children's school-related actions or inactions, interpersonal behavior (e.g., sexual behavior), fun (e.g., drinking at parties), and times of departure and arrival. The children may take offense at their parents' supervision of them. And each resists the others' imputation that their behavior is deviant. Deviance is a tool in producing and managing these conflicts.

People and social life cannot exist without the phenomenon of deviance. Therefore, look closely and think carefully about your worlds. You will see that deviance and its complexity are everywhere.

PROJECT

1. Deviance is an essential feature of social life. Groups do not exist without it. Examine closely a group in which you participate. How is deviance, the making of some behaviors, thoughts, or characteristics unacceptable, used to define your group, to establish what it is to be a member in this group? Does your group have any formal mechanisms for making what is deviant or for deciding who has committed deviance and handling those offenders? How well displayed to the members are these mechanisms? For example, are new members clearly taught the "rules" of the group? Are deviant members made an example of to other members? If the official mechanisms for punishing members are secret, do members still learn of what has been done through that official mechanism? How so? Do members use informal means, such as ridicule and ostracism, or their obverse counterparts, praise and inclusion, to shape the members' behavior and, thus, the group? How do members incorporate the standards of the group into their identities? How is deviance used within the group to enable the group to exist as a interacting collectivity of members, not as mere individuals who happen to come into one another's presence? Do not try to do all that is mentioned in this project. Use it to stimulate your investigation.

5

IT'S DISGUSTING, ISN'T IT?

People may not realize the awesome power that humans wield in making deviance. To explore that issue, I ask you to consider carefully some behaviors, which may be very difficult to do. I will start by asking you to imagine the scenario presented below. Try to place yourself in that scenario. See, hear, feel, and in other ways experience yourself in that scenario. Make it come alive for you if you can. Imagine each sentence before going to the next. Don't rush, but don't linger as you move your imagination through the scenario. *Of course*, you may stop at any point in your imagination. Whenever you stop, please write down your thoughts, feelings, and reactions. Be sure to do this once you stop.

> Imagine that you are sitting at a table across from another person. That person is your age, sex, and ethnicity. You two are pleasantly talking with each other, smiling, even laughing. When you finish, you both rise and shake hands. Then you pat each other on the back. Before departing, you hug each other. You follow the hug with kisses on each other's cheek. Next, you kiss each other on the mouth. This turns into a passionate embrace. Then, you . . .

Now, write your reactions. When you finish, continue reading.

If you reacted as many of my students have reacted to this scenario, you stopped imagining before you got to the end. By the way, what do you imagine was the end in the scenario? If you

50

reacted as many of my students have reacted, you were disgusted. You were appalled at what you were beginning to imagine. It was "sick" to imagine such intimacy with someone of the same sex. Not all of my students react this way, but most do.

How would you explain this common reaction of disgust when people imagine this scenario? Please think about this and then continue. You need not write your response.

Perhaps this reaction of disgust is common because intimacy among people of the same sex is unnatural. Therefore, people are disgusted when they imagine something that is unnatural, especially when they imagine being involved. Disgust would be a natural reaction to what is unnatural.

I believe this is a common way to make sense of the widespread reaction of disgust. Nevertheless, this explanation may misplace responsibility for our reactions and for what disgusts us.

Humans have much greater capacity to act in a wide variety of ways than we typically realize, perhaps even than we are willing to recognize. Sexuality is one of the capacities that humans have in abundance.

As Marvin Harris (1989) notes, humans have great sexuality. They are one of the sexiest animals alive. While most humans are born with a predisposition to prefer opposite-sex relations, they are not born with a "predisposition to loathe and avoid same-sex relationships" (Harris 1989, 236–37). Similarly, the small percentage of people, perhaps just a few percent, who are born with a preference for same-sex relations are not born with an aversion to opposite-sex relations. Humans are born with sexual preferences but not with sexual aversions.

Consider the Sambia of Papua New Guinea. Their society, like the societies of other people of Papua New Guinea, is based on warfare. Their society, as is typically so for societies based on warfare, is misogynist. Men are known to be inherently superior, and hostility is shown to women. Men's strength and virility, their masculinity, are obtained from other men, from their semen. It is obtained through ritualized homosexuality. This ritualized homosexuality, only part of which I present below, is part of the complex processes through which the Sambia produce and reproduce the "identities of persons, social roles, clans, and intergroup relationships across generations" (Herdt 1984, 200). Ritualized homosexuality is part of making who the Sambia are!

Young boys, from about seven to ten years old, are separated from the women and children and taken to live in an all-male hamlet for their next ten to fifteen years. During the years in the all-male hamlet, they regularly engage in homosexual activities. They first do so as the fellator in order to obtain the masculine-endowing semen from those who have it, older youths and young men. The Sambia believe that to become masculine, boys must obtain semen, and they can obtain it only from those who have it: men. The male body does not produce it. When older, they pass on their semen to the young boys as the fellated. When they marry, between the ages of eighteen and twenty-five, the young men engage in sex with their wives and with the young boys. When they become fathers, the men stop their homosexual activities with the young boys. The married men are careful not to "waste" too much of their precious semen with their wives. To do so could weaken them. Sambia men say that they prefer genital sex with their wives to oral sex with males. They also realize that "boys must at first be coerced into fellatio" (Herdt 1984, 189). Yet, preference need not entail unalterable avoidance (Herdt 1984; Harris 1989, 241; Goode 1994, 243–44).

While the Sambia permit, even require, sexual behavior that is widely unacceptable, often illegal, in many societies, they do not permit every kind of sexual behavior. For example, the older male is always to be the insertee in sexual interaction. Sambia men who sought semen from other men would be stigmatized; to seek it from boys would be "morally unconscionable" (Herdt 1984, 191). Homosexual contact among clansmen and certain others is also prohibited. Adultery by husbands and wives is condemned (Herdt 1984).

The Sambia are not the only people who engage in homosexual behavior that is approved, even expected, by their society. Many non-Western societies tolerate or even encourage some same-sex erotic behavior along with opposite-sex relations (Harris 1989, 237).

WHAT UNDERSTANDING CAN WE CREATE?

I imagine that you may have had some difficulty reading about the Sambia. Their practices are very different from what you know to be so. Their practices "are" disgusting, even revolting. Yet, what understanding can we develop from the practices of the Sambia and from our disgust in imagining the opening scenario? Please develop your reply, no matter how tentative, then continue.

I think a useful understanding is the following: Much of the deviance that we most abhor is part of the natural capacity of humans as a species of animal. The deviance that we most abhor is not alien to human nature. Further, and perhaps equally difficult to recognize, much of the deviance that we most abhor has been permitted, even encouraged or required, within some societies. Normal members of those societies engage in the behavior that many of us find most disgusting. Finally, humans have the awesome ability to transform what is part of their natural capacity into something that is an abomination, into something that is horrifyingly deviant. That ability to do so has been crucial for creating the life that a people take for granted. The description of the Sambia and their ritual sexual practices among males and the disgust that many of us experience in reaction to the practices of the Sambia and to that imagined scenario support the points I have presented above.

KILLING KIDS

Let's think about two other behaviors that we abhor. They, too, support the points I have presented. First, imagine being a parent. You have just had a child. Instead of nurturing it, you suffocate it, abandon it, or in some other way kill it. It is disgusting to imagine killing one's infant. As a father of two children, I find it hard even to write that passage.

Americans were shocked several years ago when they watched and read about the unfolding saga of the young mother in South Carolina who first claimed that her two young boys were carjacked and then later confessed to strapping them into their car seats and rolling the car into a lake. Many Americans could not imagine how a mother could do that to her *own* children. The mother must have been evil or mentally deranged, people surmised. Humans, however, have often killed their unwanted young. In hunting and gathering societies, parents kill perhaps as many as half of their newborns (Lenski, Lenski, and Nolan 1991, 99). Unwanted girls are routinely killed in some societies. In nineteenth-century China boys outnumbered girls 4–1 in some regions. Similar imbalances occurred in northern India. Europeans were horrified at how common infanticide was in Asia. Yet Europeans widely practiced it during the 1700s and 1800s, though often indirectly. Some mothers took their nursing infants to bed and "accidentally" rolled on top of them, suffocating them. Others used wetnurses to rid themselves of unwanted infants. Parents paid wetnurses to nurse their young, though the parents knew that the wetnurses would not have enough breast milk to nourish the many infants in their care. Government foundling hospitals were also used by parents to rid themselves of unwanted infants. More than 300,000 babies were left from 1824 to 1833 in France (Harris 1989, 210–14).

Infanticide is not as prevalent today in Western societies. Nevertheless, people still rid themselves of their unwanted young. They do so before the young are born! For example, in the United States, more than 1.5 million abortions are performed each year, approximately 379 abortions for every 1,000 live births (U.S. Bureau of the Census 1996, 86). Worldwide, 45 million abortions are performed annually (*The State* 1996a). I am not claiming that we should or should not do abortions. Abortions are, however, one way through which humans have routinely killed their unwanted young. Doing so is part of humans' natural capacity.

EATING PEOPLE

What could be more horrifying than killing babies? Consider drinking the blood of humans, eating their flesh and their organs.

Consider cannibalism. Does just reading these words revolt you? Americans were horrified a decade ago to learn of Jeffrey Dahmer, who killed more than a dozen young men and ate parts of some of them. Many of us know of instances of survivors of shipwrecks and airplane crashes who ate fellow survivors. But cannibalism has been much more common among humans than that due to extreme, life-threatening emergencies or extremely troubled perpetrators.

Cannibalism has been widespread among small-scale band-and-village societies and chiefdoms. These small-scale societies had difficulty feeding their members. The societies could try to limit the size of their populations or their use of resources—forests, soil and game—needed for survival. Limiting the size of their populations was difficult; limiting the use of resources would undermine their members' health. An alternative was warfare with neighboring societies. By killing or driving away members of neighboring societies, more resources would be available to the victors. Enslaving the enemy, however, simply produced more people to feed. Instead, the enemy might be eaten, which provided protein for the protein-starved people (Harris 1989, 302–4, 428–30).

But not just "primitive" people have eaten fellow humans. The flesh, blood, heart, and other parts of the human body were used for medicinal purposes from the sixteenth to the eighteenth century in England and elsewhere in Europe. Standard medical books recommended bodily parts for internal and external use. Executioners in seventeenth-century England sold the still-warm blood of decapitated criminals to customers in the crowds of thousands who assembled to applaud and jeer the criminals. While the American medical community apparently did not officially approve of the medicinal use of humans, such use was made. A minister and lay physician who lived in England until his mid-twenties, when he emigrated to Massachusetts, administered medicinal remedies made from human corpses (Gordon-Grube 1988). Humans are not naturally averse to consuming their fellow humans. Doing so can even be sacred (Harris 1989, 432–41)!

DISGUST AND RESPONSIBILITY

Humans have a great natural capacity to act in a wide variety of ways. Those behaviors that are most abhorred are part of that natural capacity. Those behaviors that people find loathsome have been permitted, even encouraged or required, by some societies. Normal members of those societies, our "ancestors" in some cases, not deranged individuals, engaged in those behaviors. Those behaviors that are most abhorred are not naturally disgusting.

Yet humans also have the capacity to turn what is part of their natural capacity into that which is abominable. By making what some societies accept, even promote, unthinkably disgusting, horrifyingly unnatural, other societies decrease dramatically the likelihood that their members will express that natural capacity. These societies have also shaped their members to be very different people than those societies that permit, even encourage, those abhorred behaviors. Consider again same-sex relations.

Students who are disgusted by the scenario of increasing intimacy that I asked you and them to imagine are not necessarily intolerant of those who are gay (though same-sex behavior and being gay are not the same, something that many of us confuse, but that I will not discuss further). Instead, many of the students say that those who are gay should be allowed to be themselves, to express their sexual identities—as long as they do not flaunt it, add some of the students. The private behavior of people is their business, claim the students. Some of the students know people who are gay; some have friends who are gay.

The students' visceral disgust when imagining being involved in that scenario of increasing intimacy contrasts starkly with their personal expression of the growing public tolerance for those who are gay. The students, as almost all of us in America, have become social beings in which same-sex sexual relations are disgusting. They "are" disgusting *because* we continue to make that so.

But I am not arguing that we should or should not try to make same-sex sexual behavior, infanticide, cannibalism, or any other abhorred behavior that is part of the natural capacity of humans acceptable for us. I am not arguing that we should tolerate or promote the expression of all that comes naturally to humans. (And a people cannot simply decide tomorrow to promote a behavior that it has long made, often without realizing it, unthinkingly disgusting. That disgust is embedded in the way of life of that people. Fundamental change is not so simple.) Not at all. I have no desire for us to champion the enslavement of humans, the burning of dissidents at the stake, the casual slaughter of enemies, the ritual sacrifice of children, and other atrocities (at least those acts are atrocious to me) that humans have routinely done and, in some cases, still do.

Instead, I am encouraging us to take together responsibility for what disgusts us. Perhaps it is too frightening for us to accept what I have presented above. It is certainly more comforting to act as if some behaviors are naturally loathsome, alien to normal human nature, than to recognize the fundamental, continuing challenge that all people face. The challenge is to confront the capacity of human nature and to decide what of that capacity will be tolerated, accepted, promoted, discouraged, prohibited, made abominable. Nature cannot do that for us, no matter how much we may appeal to it. We are left to confront who we become.

CONCLUSION

Well, are homosexuality, infanticide, and eating people disgusting? I encourage you to think further about what a people make disgusting, even if it is not made to be as abominable as the three topics I discussed. Who is making the behaviors, thoughts, or characteristics disgusting? What meanings are used to make the behaviors, thoughts, or characteristics disgusting? What are the consequences of making these disgusting? How do people draw the line between what is disgusting and what is not? How do other groups of people handle these behaviors, thoughts, and characteristics? What is not being made disgusting?

For example, sexual activities with someone who is "under age" is illegal—and to many of us quite repugnant. (And I am not saying that it should not be repugnant.) If the person is one day older, however, then the same sexual activity is legal. In other societies, Iraq, for example, marriage and sexual activities with young girls may be quite common (Annin and Hamilton, 1996). Apparently many Japanese men legally turn sexually to schoolgirls over whom they feel in control. Yet an editor of a magazine that presents pictures of naked schoolgirls says that only "maniacs" go for girls below the third grade (*The State* 1997c). Even in early America the age of consent for girls was ten (Goodman 1996).

To think about what is made disgusting is not intended to undermine what is cherished and what is abhorred. Instead, to think about what is made disgusting is to take seriously the responsibility that people have for living and acting together, for creating their worlds.

PROJECTS

1. If you dare, take the scenario that opens this chapter and present it to people you know. Ask them to write their reactions to it. Then ask them to explain their reactions. If people find that opening scenario disgusting, as I believe most will, why do they? Do they assume that such behavior is unnatural or an abomination against what the divine has decreed? Or ask people to respond to the other topics presented—infanticide and cannibalism. What are people's responses and their explanations for their responses? Do many, perhaps most, people take for granted that such behaviors are unnatural or an abomination?

2. Through searching books and articles, explore how other behaviors or conditions that are widely taken to be disgusting by your society have been tolerated, accepted, or even promoted or required by other social groups or societies. How did those societies understand these practices that disgust us, but not them? For example, some forms of punishment we consider barbaric were or are routinely used by other people. Or explore what other people take to be unnatural that your society may find quite acceptable. For example, eating beef would be an abomination to Hindus, but many Americans apparently cannot eat enough hamburgers or steaks. How do Hindus understand the eating of beef?

To a lesser extent, one group may make deviant a particular behavior that another group accepts. The first group does not make the deviant behavior abominable, just unacceptable. The second group thinks nothing of it. Explore groups within your local worlds, such as sororities and fraternities, different college classes, stores, and such. Investigate how two groups may treat the same behavior quite differently.

6

IS DEVIANCE HARMFUL OR HELPFUL?

Is deviance harmful or helpful? What do you think? Are sexual assault, academic cheating, robbery, mental health problems, underage drinking, sexually explicit material, failure to pay organizational dues, gang violence, violating work rules, governmental misconduct, corporate fraud, and much more destructive or constructive? Think of your deviance. Is it harmful or helpful? Please take some time to consider this issue, then write your response. When you are finished, continue reading.

   The question is more complex than one might imagine. To address it, we might need to consider to whom deviance might be harmful or helpful, for what might it be harmful or helpful, when might it be harmful or helpful, and other issues. Perhaps we should explore whether specific kinds of deviance are harmful or helpful. In this chapter I do not explore all of that complexity. Instead, I urge you to think about deviance in some nonobvious ways.

HARMFUL DEVIANCE

Deviance certainly can be harmful. Did you list ways in which deviance may be harmful? For example, drug use may damage users, murder ends life, robbery makes the victim poorer, and abuse traumatizes. Shoplifting and employee theft costs businesses and the public hundreds of billions of dollars annually (Hogsett and Radig 1994). Through violations of workplace safety regulations or academic cheating, people create unfair advantages for themselves to the detriment of others. In these obvious ways, deviance harms the offender, the victim, and other people.

Deviance can also harm social life. It can damage the ability of people to live and act together adequately. The colleague who drinks, the spouse who has mental health problems, and the committee member who sexually harasses staff make it difficult for the work group, the family, and the committee to function well. The same is so if a group is deviant. Its deviance may make it more difficult for the larger organization to perform adequately. Rogue police officers may taint the entire department.

Deviance may lessen conventional people's willingness to abide by the rules, to do their part, to contribute their share. If conventional people see that others are getting away with inappropriate behavior, then they may become resentful. They may question the fairness of what is happening. If cheating goes undetected or unpunished to the benefit of the cheaters, then more students may cheat. If co-workers goof off, then other workers may resent the extra work they must do.

Most important, deviance undermines, even destroys, trust among people. Confidence in others to do what is expected, the assurance that one can depend on others, solidarity among people, all may be damaged through deviance. Parents become wary of their teenage children who deceive them. Spouses break up over unfaithfulness. After a rash of shoplifting, sales managers and staff become suspicious of shoppers, straining the relation with customers. Teachers eye students like a hawk during exams. Victims of crime, such as mugging or sexual assault, may develop a pervasive unease that accompanies them everywhere they go (LeJeune and Alex 1973; Allison and Wrightsman 1993: chap. 8). Without trust, it becomes difficult to do anything with others (Collins 1992: chap. 1). One is always on guard (Cohen 1966, 4–6). Deviance can harm people and their ability to live and act with one another.

HELPFUL DEVIANCE

But can deviance be helpful? Certainly. Some deviance can give advantage to the offender. Predatory crimes such as robbery or burglary, plagiarism, cheating, employee theft, corporate fraud, embezzlement, violation of workplace safety regulations, and many other forms of deviance benefit the successful perpetrator. This is obvious. Other benefits to the perpetrator may be less obvious. I briefly discuss that point in chapter 9.

But can deviance benefit more than the offender? Can it benefit those who are not deviant? Can it *contribute* to social life? I and others think it can (Black 1983; Cohen 1966; Collins 1992; Coser 1962; Davis 1937; Dentler and Erikson 1959; Durkheim 1966; Erikson 1962; Mead 1918). How do you think deviance could be constructive for, not just destructive of, social life? Please develop some possibilities, then continue reading. I now explore some of the ways in which deviance may be constructive.

The first ways I mention in which deviance can be beneficial are less important for social life, though certainly significant to the people directly affected. Deviance is *big business* for conventional people. Millions of correctional officers, police officers, attorneys, social workers, juvenile justice staff, mental health professionals, drug-abuse counselors, and others make a living from deviance. So do professors who teach, research, and write about deviance! Hundreds of billions of dollars are spent yearly to deal with deviance. Of course, that takes away from spending on other possible projects not related to deviance or from the taxpayer who might be taxed less. Community officials compete to have correctional facilities, mental health institutions, or other agencies that deal with deviance located in their communities because the "deviance facilities" may provide needed jobs and economic development. Are you employed or are you planning to work in the legitimate side of the big business of deviance? Do you know anyone who is? I imagine that you do.

Deviance is an important feature in the *media*—in news and entertainment. Deviance helps fill news space. Recall the deviance items with which I began the introduction to this book. It is used to sell the news and entertainment media. Deviance entertains us. Perhaps we get a vicarious thrill through learning of others' deviance. Think about what programs and movies you watch and what books, magazines, and news stories you read. I imagine that many of them concern deviance. You might investigate how extensively and prominently the media display deviance. You may be surprised.

More important, I think, deviance contributes in various ways to social life, to the ability of some people to live and act together adequately. As I explained in a previous chapter, deviance is an essential feature of social life. Through deviance, through the power of making unacceptable some forms of human existence, people structure social life. They give meaning to who they are. They instruct one another about how to act. They give feeling to experience. Through deviance, people try to meet the challenges of living and acting together when nothing dictates how they will act.

Deviance makes clearer where the *boundaries of acceptability* are. For example, a teacher may expect that students will not talk too loudly or disrupt class. But what is too-loud talk or disruption? When a teacher warns or punishes students, the teacher is making clearer to all, at least for the moment, what is acceptable and what is not. When a police department cracks down on street prostitution, it (and the community) may be signaling to those involved that they have become too brazen in their behavior. They need to become more circumspect in their sexual transactions. Deviance can become a concrete example that makes clearer more abstract values and standards.

Deviance enables people and groups of all kinds to establish, even enhance, their *moral worth*. By contrasting themselves to *those* deviants, people and groups tell themselves that they are not like those others (making the boundaries of individual and group identity clearer) and that they are better than those others. The well-behaving young children feel superior to the children singled out for misbehaving. The citizens of a small town with little crime feel safer and superior to those in the dangerous big city. Of course, in enhancing one's own moral worth, one is also lessening the moral worth of others.

(Likewise, those who commit deviance may use their deviance to set themselves apart from, even superior to, those who do not commit deviance. Those who commit deviance may create part of their identity in contrast to those who are conventional. Those who commit deviance may view those who are conventional as square, lame, or in other derisive ways.)

Deviance provides an opportunity for people to *strengthen solidarity* among themselves. Through reacting in similar ways toward the deviant—with outrage, horror, pity, disgust, fright, amusement, and so on—people create shared experiences and feelings. Through collaborating to deal with the deviant and deviance—perhaps to punish, to reform, to prevent—those who are not deviant join in a common purpose that can unite them. They may be united against the deviant or even with the deviant. Colleagues may work together to help a co-worker who has a problem with drinking. Family members may unite to try to help another family member who has a drug problem, eventually bringing that troubled family member closer to them. A neighborhood group may organize itself to stop a rash of burglaries. An entire country may grow more cohesive to defend itself against a hostile country. Deviance can provide an enemy against which to rally, or it can provide troubled people to assist and problems to tackle.

Change may be produced through deviance. Some deviance directly challenges the legitimacy of the present social order, the conventional ways of doing things. If successful, the deviance has been a catalyst for creating new ways of living and acting together. New fashion may be initially considered unacceptable and only later become quite conventional. Same, too, with musical, literary, and other artistic efforts. Unconventional work that is despised, even banned, may later revolutionize the field. Scientific advancement may be produced through scientists challenging the present understandings and ways of doing science. Certainly the civil rights movement of the 1950s and 1960s, which challenged the unequal legal status of African Americans, led to important changes in America. That is true also in other countries where civil protest has occurred, such as South Africa. The American and South African protesters were deviant. The defenders of the status quo reacted harshly, sometimes violently, toward the protesters. But their protests became catalysts for significant social change (Higgins and Butler 1982, 231–35; Morris 1984).

Deviance can be constructive for social life. I explored several ways in which it can be: as big business, in the media, for establishing the boundaries of acceptability and doing so concretely, for moral worth, and as a catalyst for social change. Deviance is more complex than we typically imagine. To end this discussion, I briefly discuss the ambivalence that low-income communities experience about gangs in their communities. That ambivalence points in specific ways to how deviance can be constructive, not destructive, of social life.

CONCLUSION: COMMUNITIES' AMBIVALENCE TOWARD GANGS

I believe that we can readily understand when communities organize to oppose gang activity or ask for the police to do something, but we may be surprised when communities appear to tolerate gang activity or complain that the police are too forceful in their response (Jankowski 1991, 317–18). Residents of low-income communities may be ambivalent about gangs. Certainly they oppose the destruction and harm caused by gangs. But their responses to gangs and their feelings about gangs are more complex.

Part of the ambivalence is the good that community residents see coming from gangs. Gangs provide *protection* from others, including other gangs, who would prey on the residents. Having existed for years, perhaps even decades, the gangs have become *social institutions* in the communities. They provide a means for low-income boys, and perhaps girls, to make the "rite of passage to adulthood" (Jankowski 1991, 318). Finally, residents may believe that without a so-called gang problem, city officials and other authorities would provide few *resources* or give little attention to the neighborhoods.

Deviance does harm. But it may also help. It may help not only the offender but also conventional citizens. In the next chapter I explore how deviance may not only help social life but may be the opposite of what it is commonly taken to be. How is the deviance in your social world harmful? How is it helpful?

PROJECTS

1. Deviance may not only harm social life, it may also help. Deviance may be big business for conventional people. Many people work legitimately in the deviance arena as police officers, social workers, drug counselors, and in other ways. Explore how important deviance is in your community for providing legitimate work. Contact those agencies that in some way manage deviance—police departments, mental health agencies, child protection units of social service departments, judicial courts, private security companies, and so on. Learn how many people work in those various agencies, offices, and companies. This procedure will overlook people who work in deviance but do so within agencies that otherwise do not focus on deviance, such as a drug specialist for a large school district. Obtain the number of people employed in your community from your local government. What percentage of employees work in the deviance business? How important is deviance for your community?

The flip side of this employment in deviance is that money spent on the employees and their agencies could be used elsewhere if not spent on deviance. If budgets are available, try to calculate how much money is spent in your community on deviance. You may be able to obtain budgets from your local and state governments. Examine the budgets to see how much is appropriated for those agencies and offices that primarily deal with deviance. What percentage of the governments' budgets is spent on deviance?

2. If a present episode of deviance and its handling is occurring in a group of which you are a member, or a recent one has occurred, investigate how that episode and its handling contributes (or contributed) to the production or destruction of social life. For example, are conventional members creating conflict among one another concerning how the offender and the offense should be handled? Or are they creating common interests concerning the deviance, and thereby creating greater solidarity among themselves? Perhaps through the deviance and their reaction to it, members of the group have made clearer to one another what is and is not acceptable. What have been the consequences of the episode of deviance for the group?

7

CAN DEVIANCE BE INTENDED TO
PROMOTE MORALITY, NOT VIOLATE IT?

We may profit from viewing deviance in ways other than it is commonly seen. Instead of being an attack against what is acceptable, deviance may be intended to promote what is appropriate. We may usefully think of deviance as a means of social control. We may view deviance in other ways, too, as I suggest at the end of this chapter.

Consider basketball. Perhaps you have played it, are at present playing it, or enjoy watching it. If you can, imagine that you are playing in a game. An opponent begins to shove, push, elbow, or in other ways play "dirty" or rough against you. You tell the opponent to stop it, but the opponent does not do so. As the referees apparently don't see it, you let them know what the opponent is doing. But the referees do nothing about it. Maybe one of them even tells you to stop complaining and just play. What might you do? Why? Please write your response, then continue.

Let me present another scenario. Imagine that you are back in elementary school. A classmate annoys you by messing with your papers, pencils, books, and other school materials. You tell the classmate to cut it out, but the classmate messes with your things later that day and the next day. You continue to tell the classmate to stop, but the classmate doesn't. You do not go to your teacher because the teacher has told the class not to tattle on classmates. What might you do and why? Please write your response, then continue.

I wonder if you decided to handle both scenarios in ways that may have been deviant, but for which you had good reason. Return to the basketball game. Did you, as basketball players at times do when in the same situation, retaliate against the opponent who pushed, shoved, elbowed, or in other ways played dirty against you? Did you shove the opponent, surreptiously grab the opponent, or in other ways block the movement of the opponent? If you did, then you may have been whistled for a foul, as are players who do that in actual games. Were you seeking an unfair advantage, or were you trying to get the opponent to play fair?

The actual, retaliating players who are called for their fouls are not necessarily seeking unfair advantage. Instead, frustrated by the continuing dirty play of opponents, the players take matters into their own hands. They are not trying to undermine the standards of the game, the fairness of the competition. Instead, they are trying to uphold the standards and the fairness. But their attempts to do so are whistled as deviant by the referees.

Consider again the annoying classmate. How did you handle that scenario? After not succeeding in asking the classmate to stop, did you take matters into your own hands? Did you give the annoying classmate an ultimatum and then back it up if the classmate continued? Perhaps you took something of the classmate's, messed with some of the classmate's things, or in other ways retaliated against the classmate. If you did so, is it because you were trying to disrupt the classroom or because you were trying to uphold appropriate conduct among students in the classroom? And if you retaliated, you can certainly imagine that the teacher may have seen you and punished you for *your* misbehavior.

In both scenarios, you may have acted in ways taken to be deviant by those in charge—the referees or the teacher. You may have been punished in consequential ways. Yet you were not trying to undermine the standards of the basketball game or the classroom. Instead, you were trying to uphold morality. Much deviance, even serious deviance such as crime, may be usefully understood as attempts to promote the standards of the group, not undermine them.

DEVIANCE AS SOCIAL CONTROL

Donald Black (1983) argues that much crime, even serious predatory crime, can be understood as self-help attempts to control the
deviance of others when formal means of social control are perceived to be inadequate (or unnecessary). Much serious deviance
is social control.

Consider running away. Much of it is done when youths can
no longer put up with the perceived unacceptable behavior of
their families or their school teachers and officials. Committing
this juvenile delinquency is their attempt to right the wrong
(Black 1983, 38; Ek and Steelman 1988).

Look at vandalism. Some observers think vandalism is done
without purpose. But people may vandalize property because
they believe the owners have offended them. Perhaps a driver has
parked in a curb-side parking place cleared of snow by someone
else but knows that the one who clears the space has, by custom,
the right to use it (Black 1983, 37). Maybe a business owner re-
fuses to hire local youths for summer employment, even ha-
rassing them when they enter the owner's establishment. A
neighbor may have threatened to call the police on some youth
who are innocently standing and talking good-naturedly and
loudly on the sidewalk outside the neighbor's house. In all these
situations, vandalism may be committed as a response to the perceived injustice of what was done earlier by the "victim" of the
vandalism.

Even predatory offenses may be attempts to uphold community standards, not violate them. An older brother may beat up
someone who has bothered his sister. An individual may illegally
enter a former roommate's apartment to get back disputed property, especially when the ex-roommate stiffed the individual with
back rent. Robberies may concern disputes over money and other
valuables among acquaintances. Even murder, as I explore in another chapter, may be an attempt to reassert one's honor and dignity in the face of what is experienced as overwhelming,
never-ending disrespect (Katz 1988, chap. 1).

People may resort to deviant, even criminal, self-help when
they perceive that the formal means of addressing disputes have

not worked or are not available or appropriate for them. For example, parents and teachers may not intervene when siblings or classmates have disputes with one another. The siblings or classmates may then use deviant self-help. Or the law is not readily available for participants to settle disputes concerning gambling debts, drug sales, transactions in prostitution, and other forms of illegal acts. Those involved in illegal activities may use illegal self-help in order to achieve justice.

Some people more than others may have experienced or believe that formal or conventional means for managing disputes are not readily available. Who do you think may more likely believe that formal, conventional means for managing disputes are not readily available to them?

Those with less status—poor people, minority citizens, those who live on the streets, and the young among others—may not have as much access to the police and other formal means of handling disputes as those with more resources, or at least they may believe that they do not. Officials may not take as seriously the complaints of people with relatively little status. Similarly, those in intimate relations, such as spouses, may come to see that their disputes will be treated as private matters to be avoided by officials, not public matters for officials to handle. Consequently, they may handle disputes among themselves, instead of unsatisfactorily summoning law enforcement. In all these situations and more, people may use deviant self-help to promote justice, to uphold community standards. Ironically, deviance, that which people make to be unacceptable, may be done in order to stop or punish the offensive behavior of others (Black 1983).

Deviant self-help may constitute a social movement instead of being the response of individuals to their own perceived injustices. The civil rights protests in America and South Africa certainly attempted to extend what a society held dear to segments of the citizenry that believed they had been denied those rights and benefits. Those civil rights movements were taken to be deviant by many officials and citizens. The movements were countered with violence by some officials and by some ordinary citizens.

Is deviant self-help, then, noble? Not necessarily. Much of it may create great harm. People are hurt or killed; property is damaged or taken. I am not urging people to take matters into their hands. But when people do, when they use deviant self-help to redress perceived wrongs, the community at times may be more tolerant of them and their deviance than it would be otherwise. For example, behavior that could readily be seen as assault is less likely to lead to an arrest when the combatants are intimately related than when they are strangers. Presumably combatants known to one another are addressing perceived wrongs (Black 1983, 40).

CONCLUSION

Instead of a violation of morality, deviance may be understood as an attempt to uphold morality. We may usefully understand deviance in still other ways. How else might we understand deviance?

Some deviance may be appropriately understood as recreation. For example, the deviant use of drugs may have much in common with the legal use of alcohol. Both may be part of creating a "good time." Crime, then, becomes play or leisure activity (Richards, Berk, and Forster 1979). Other deviance can be understood as economic behavior. For example, fencing stolen merchandise may be more similar to retail sales than to assaults, drug use, or other kinds of deviance (Black 1983; Klockars 1974; Letkemann 1973; Plate 1975). Graffitti artists may be committing a crime, but they may also be creating art. Tattooing is illegal in some jurisdictions, and body marking and piercing are deviant to many people. Yet body marking may be similar to other means of self-presentation, group affiliation, even spiritual awakening (Hewitt 1997, chap. 4).

If we view deviance as leisure activity, economic behavior, art, self-presentation, or in other ways, then we need to explore deviance differently. We need to raise questions about deviance that we would raise about other leisure activities, economic behavior, and so on. For example, if we view drug production and distribution as economic behavior, then we may explore the social organization of how drugs are produced, how dealers obtain their stock, how customers are developed, how sales are made, and much more (Adler 1985; Inciardi 1992).

Deviance may be more than we first imagine it to be. That which offends at least some people is deviance. But deviance may also be usefully understood as a means of social control, play, economic behavior, perhaps even artistic expression, and still other forms of behavior. How else do you think we might usefully understand deviance?

I encourage you to think about the deviance that you commit and about the deviance done by others of which you are aware. Is it useful to think about that deviance as something more than, even other than, that which is offensive?

PROJECT

1. Through talking with people who have committed deviance, investigate what morality, if any, the offenders believed they were trying to uphold through their deviance. Was their deviance a means for controlling or responding to the offensive actions of others? For example, perhaps someone committed employee theft in response to the perceived unfair treatment received from the manager. Talk with people who have committed assault, employee deviance, shoplifting, or other deviance. The people who have committed the deviance may provide self-serving justifications for their actions. I believe it may be difficult to make a useful distinction between a self-serving justification and a sincerely presented account of the moral good the offenders thought they were protecting. Media stories of deviance may present offenders' accounts of their behaviors that also can be examined for the moral good that the offenders believed they were upholding. What are your reactions to these "morality tales"?

8

HOW MUCH DEVIANCE IS THERE?

How much deviance is there? Please think about this question, then continue. Did you think a lot, more than in the past, too much, you don't know, or the like? You could not be expected to know the exact amount of deviance. You are not likely to know the latest statistics on deviance. Neither would I, until I searched for them.

Why should we be concerned about how much deviance there is? We should be concerned because we and others use deviance statistics. They are important in our lives, even if we do not realize it (Pfuhl and Henry 1993, chap. 2). Let me present some headlines from my city's newspaper about deviance, in particular about crime. What is your reaction to these headlines? After thinking about the headlines, continue reading my discussion of the significance of deviance statistics.

"Teen Drug Use Soaring, Survey Finds" (*The State* 1996f)."
"Study Records Decline in Crime" (*The State* 1997d).
"Is School Crime On the Rise?" (Patterson 1998).

First, statistics are taken by many of us as "hard" information. People's statements are "just" their opinions; numbers are the facts. While perhaps nowadays we are more skeptical, even cynical, than in the past, many of us still take statistics as telling us what is so, if not completely so (Pfuhl and Henry 1993 27–28). For example, did you interpret the headlines presented above as if the statistics (or implied statistics) told you what were the facts? Or did you react cautiously, skeptically, to the statistics?

Second, to the extent that we take statistics as factual, then we may use them to tell us about the moral order of our world (Pfuhl and Henry 1993, 28). How moral or decadent is our world? How safe is it? Is the world worsening or improving? Deviance statistics not only tell us how much deviance exists, but the statistics may also tell us where deviance is most likely to occur, who is most likely to commit deviance, and other information. We may become more or less fearful, more or less morally concerned about our world or about segments of it, because of statistics, the stories based on them, and our interpretation of the statistics and stories (Liska and Baccaglini 1990; Beckett 1994). When reading the newspaper headlines listed above, did you feel that the world was less safe, more safe, even less or more moral?

Third, researchers and citizens use statistics on deviance to develop, evaluate, and decide about explanations for the causes of deviance (Pfuhl and Henry 1993, 28). For example, if we interpret statistics of deviance to show that those who are impoverished commit more deviance than those who are not impoverished, as statistics often have been interpreted, then we may develop theories trying to explain why that is so (Merton 1957). Finally, government officials and service providers use statistics in developing and proposing legislation and programs to combat deviance, requesting and allocating funds for programs to combat deviance, and evaluating the results of the programs (Pfuhl and Henry 1993, 29). We might think about how much deviance there is (and about other issues concerning the amount) because deviance statistics do make a difference in our lives.

Once again, how much deviance is there? What do you think? That is not a good question. It is much too general. I need to specify the kinds of deviance, the location, the time period, and even more qualifications before addressing the question. Let me rephrase the question, make it more specific, and bring it closer to "home." How much crime occurred on your college campus in the past year? How do you know?

At the University of South Carolina in Columbia, where I teach, 615 violent crimes and property crimes occurred in a recent year. You might ask how I know. The FBI's *Uniform Crime Reports* (*UCR*) tells me so (Federal Bureau of Investigation 1995,

163). You can look at that report to see how much crime has occurred on your college campus. How does the FBI know? Since 1929, the FBI has collected information on crimes known to local law enforcement agencies through its *UCR* Program. Since the late 1980s, colleges and universities receiving federal funds have been required by federal law to collect and report information on crime on their campuses. The FBI collects information on the violent crimes of homicide, forcible rape, robbery, and aggravated assault and on property crimes of burglary, larceny-theft, motor vehicle theft, and arson. The bureau calls this its crime index. The bureau collects but presents much less information on other crimes, such as embezzlement, drug-abuse violations, gambling, forgery, and drunkenness.

OFFICIALLY COUNTING DEVIANCE

The FBI's *UCR* statistics are *official counts* of deviance. Local law enforcement agencies collect, record, and present information about the crimes and criminals that they officially handle. Many other agencies also record official counts of deviance. Departments of mental health collect official counts of those who have mental health troubles. Divisions of natural resources or wildlife in state governments may record official counts of those who violate wildlife regulations. Offices of student affairs or disciplinary boards at colleges collect official counts of student infractions of the colleges' regulations. Departments of social services prepare official counts of child abuse. School officials formally record statistics on student deviance. Many agencies provide official counts of deviance, and the media may report them. The last of the three headlines presented at the beginning of this chapter is based on an official count.

Do you have any questions about these official counts of deviance? I imagine that you may object to using the *UCR* information to know how much crime has occurred on your campus. Likewise, you may object to using official counts of all kinds to know how much deviance exists. Why may you object to using official counts of deviance? Please formulate your response before continuing.

You may object that many crimes are not reported to the police. Therefore, the *UCR* information is not accurate. Likewise, you may object that many people with mental health difficulties do not come to the attention of officials within departments of mental health, that violations of wildlife laws are not always known by wildlife enforcement agencies, that students may violate the regulations of their colleges without authorities finding out, that much child abuse never comes to the attention of social service agencies, and that school officials may be clueless about students' deviance. This is an important objection made by many critics of official counts.

If official counts are not accurate, then how else could we count deviance? If you are not satisfied with the FBI's official record of crime at your college, then what could be done to learn how much crime has occurred at your college? Why don't you list some possibilities before continuing.

UNOFFICIALLY COUNTING DEVIANCE

Perhaps you thought of one or both of two ways that I next explore. Both have been widely used for learning the amount of different kinds of deviance, information about who commits it, and other related information.

First, students could be asked to report about their criminal behavior at college for the past year (or any time period of interest). For example, a questionnaire that asks students to report on their commission of crimes listed on the questionnaire could be distributed to students (or a sample of students). This is a *self-report* study. The students report about their criminal behavior. Scholars use self-report methods to learn how much crime people commit, about people's sexual behavior (some of which is deviant), about their mental health difficulties, about deviance they have committed against their employers, about academic dishonesty, and much more. People can report their deviance through distributed questionnaires, in face-to-face interviews, by telephone, or in other ways.

Do you have any questions about this self-report method? Perhaps you wonder whether people will be honest in their reporting. Social scientists have checked this possibility with mixed results. For example, youths will report committing crimes, they will report crimes not known to officials, and they are very likely to report crimes known to officials. But those who have high rates of official delinquency are less likely than those with low rates of official delinquency to admit to crimes known to the police (Hindelang, Hirschi, and Weis 1981, chap. 11). Self-reports may work best for counting the deviance of those who are least seriously involved.

Do you have other questions? I imagine so. You might object that people forget. People forget they committed some deviance, how much deviance they committed, when they committed deviance, and so on. No doubt, that occurs. Researchers know this. Therefore, investigators may ask people to report about their recent behavior if they are trying to obtain a specific count of deviance.

You may also object that even if college students honestly respond about their criminal conduct, the count will still be inaccurate. It will be inaccurate because some crimes committed on college campuses are committed by people who are not students. And some crimes committed by the students are committed away from their colleges. Good point. Self-report counts cover the deviance of a group of people better than the deviance in a particular place.

If we do not use self-reports to learn how much crime occurred on a college campus, what could we do? We could ask students to report about their victimization. For example, have the students been a victim of crime on their college campuses in the past year? Here you may raise some of the same objections that you did to self-report counts. Students may not wish to admit that they were victimized. Citizens who are not students may have been victimized on the campus. Some students may have forgotten being a victim. For example, they may have forgotten being in a fight. Crimes such as drug use or underage drinking would not be reported because no victims are involved. And so on. Again, scholars are aware of these concerns and try to handle them carefully when using victimization surveys.

Victimization surveys are used to explore crime, sexual harassment, domestic abuse, and other deviance in which people are victimized. For example, since 1973, the Bureau of Justice Statistics has conducted the National Crime Survey, now called the National Crime Victimization Survey (NCVS). U.S. Census Bureau personnel interview approximately 100,000 people twelve years of age and older in a sample of approximately 49,000 households. The households remain in the sample for three years and are interviewed every six months about their victimization (Federal Bureau of Investigation 1994, Appendix IV). The second headline mentioned at the beginning of this chapter is based on the National Crime Victimization Survey.

These self-report and victimization studies produce *unofficial counts* of crime and deviance. The counts are not based on the records of official agencies that handle people who have committed crimes or deviance. They are obtained through individuals' reporting their criminal or deviant conduct or their victimization of such. Even though a federal agency, the Bureau of Justice Statistics, conducts the NCVS, the count it obtains is unofficial. Certainly, some crime and deviance that are reported on self-report studies and on victimizations surveys have been officially recorded. But official counts are based on the records of official agencies. Unofficial counts are obtained through the responses of people.

WHICH METHOD SHOWS MORE?

Which method, official or unofficial, do you think provides the larger count? Scholars agree that unofficial methods provide the larger count, sometimes much larger. For example, the *UCR* reported 660,000 robberies for 1993 (Federal Bureau of Investigation 1994, 26). The NCVS reported 1.3 million robberies (Perkins, Klaus, Bastian, and Cohen 1996, 9).

You can "see" this result for yourself. Ask friends to report whether they have committed several kinds of deviance within a particular time period (e.g., within the past year, at college, or since entering high school). If they have, then ask them to report how much they have committed. For this demonstration, you need not try to be precise. You could ask them to give you a definite figure or you could ask them to estimate their involvement. Perhaps they have committed the particular deviance a few times, several times a week, often, or some other frequency. Of course, if we wished to be precise, then we would not use such vague categories. When friends have committed a particular form of deviance, ask them whether they know of any official records that exist about their involvement in that deviance for the same time period as the self-report. Arrest records and disciplinary board hearings might be two kinds of official records that exist for some of the friends. If official records do exist, then how many exist for each particular kind of deviance? This is a simple, indirect way to obtain official counts of your friends' deviance to compare to their self-report counts.

I often ask my students to ask their friends about cheating in school, assaults of others (i.e., fights), alcohol violations, shoplifting, and other forms of deviance. What do you think my students' investigations show? They show that many of their friends have committed the various kinds of deviance that we explore, sometimes quite often. Yet very few of the friends know of any official record of their deviance. Unofficial counts show much more deviance than official counts do.

PRODUCING COUNTS

Let's return to the question that opened this chapter: how much deviance is there? How do you now reply? Perhaps it is difficult to respond. You realize that neither official nor unofficial counts present the "true," complete amount of deviance. (Those counts do not for a fundamental reason more complex than I have explored here. I take up that reason as I explore another puzzling issue in deviance in chapter 11.) Yet people do collect and use official and unofficial counts of deviance. Those counts matter, too, as I discussed earlier.

I think a useful response is this: *For all practical purposes,* as much deviance exists as officials, researchers, and other interested parties *produce* through their official or unofficial procedures. No amount exists until someone produces that amount. *Once produced, the amount becomes how much deviance there is for those who use the statistics and other information.* Important questions such as the following can then be asked: How are official and unofficial counts produced? Can they be produced otherwise? Are they useful for the purposes to which they are put? I do not take up all of these and other questions. Instead, I end this chapter on a brief discussion of how official counts of deviance are produced. If we are to use wisely official counts of deviance (as well as unofficial counts), we may wish to know how they come to exist.

Official counts of deviance are socially created (Kitsuse and Cicourel 1963). As officials and citizens manage their concerns, they produce official counts of deviance. If they change their concerns or how they manage their concerns, then they may produce different official counts (McCleary, Nienstedt, and Erven 1982). For example, the official count of 615 violent and property crimes at the University of South Carolina in Columbia during 1994 would have been produced through the following or similar actions.

First, the state legislature made illegal the acts that constitute the violent and property crimes. A law enforcement agency was created and staffed at the university to handle those offenses and other matters. Students and others on campus acted in ways to which someone took offense. Property may have been missing; cars may seemingly have been broken into; students and others may have pushed, shoved, and struck one another; people may have apparently used or threatened to use force to take property or cash from others; and so on. These offensive acts were interpreted by individuals as requiring the intervention of the university law enforcement officials. Perhaps while patrolling the campus, police officers noticed some of the events. More likely, victims or witnesses reported the events to the campus police. The police decided to investigate. Law enforcement officials do not typically investigate all matters that come to their attention.

The campus police concluded that crimes had occurred and wrote official reports. The crimes in the reports were coded as specific crimes and recorded (then sent to the FBI for inclusion in its *Uniform Crime Reports*). Many officials, students, and others produced that official count of 615 violent and property crimes through their actions.

To understand how the official count of 615 violent and property crimes came to exist, we would need to explore each of those actions. Listing them is not enough. We would need to know how people created the concerns that they have and how and why they managed their concerns as they did to produce each of those actions. If the parties involved change how they manage their concerns, then the official count may change, too. For example, if the police change their patrol practices, they may notice more or less behavior about which they become suspicious. If students become more willing to report unwanted sexual behavior, then the official counts may change. If the university changes its prevention and awareness programs concerning crime, the official counts may change. If the university reduces the student drinking on campus, then the amount of damaged property, assaults, unwanted sexual actions, and other behavior toward which students and others may take offense may decrease (Wechsler et al. 1994). Legislators, university officials, students, and others produce the official counts of college crime as they manage their concerns.

ORGANIZATIONAL PRACTICES AND THE PRODUCTION OF OFFICIAL CRIME COUNTS

Consider briefly how organizational practices in law enforcement agencies lead to the production of official crime counts (McCleary, Nienstedt, and Erven 1982). Changes in these organizational practices may lead to changes in the production of official counts of crime.

In one major southwestern city, when sergeants were removed from supervising the dispatch bureau of the police department, the number of "service calls" increased greatly, as did the official crime. A service call is a "citizen call for assistance which results in the dispatch of an officer to the scene" (McCleary, Nienstedt, and Erven 1982, 367). If a citizen calls the police department for service, but the dispatcher does not dispatch an officer to the scene, then no official crime will be recorded at that time. If the dispatcher receives an inquiry about sanitation or a call that reports a crime in progress, then the dispatcher is quite certain whether or not to dispatch an officer to the scene. But other calls appear questionable to dispatchers. For example, a call reporting that an auto has been stolen may be a repossession by the finance company or a towaway. A call reporting a burglary may be a civil matter among disputing family members. These calls appear not to concern threats to safety nor are they urgent to the police department. They are not serious, "real" crimes. Dispatchers are reluctant to send officers to the scenes in such cases. If they cannot reach a compromise with the caller, such as referring the caller to some other public agency, the dispatcher will turn to the supervising sergeant. Dispatchers do that, in part, to protect themselves from civil suits, internal investigations, or other consequences. When sergeants were removed from supervising dispatchers, the dispatchers were left without this important protection. Hence, they increased their likelihood of dispatching officers to the scenes of the calls. With an increase in officers being dispatched, the official counts of crime increased.

In a police department in another southwestern city, the official count of burglaries increased 20 percent during the second half of the year after a formal job offer was made to the police chief. News of the retirement spread quickly through the police department, though it was kept hidden from the public for many months. The shake-up in the administration caused by the retirement directly affected the coding of incident reports by clerks in the coding bureau. The coding bureau was supervised by a sergeant, who reported to a commander of the research and planning division. The commander reported to an assistant chief. All three were replaced in the shake-up. Before the commander left, he was not around the department as much as he typically had been. Perhaps he was looking for a new job. Even when the commander was at the department, he did not spend as much time in the office.

The commander demanded that coding be done his way, even if some of the guidelines he used may have been wrong. He let coders know if they had not done it his way. If coders were uncertain, then they were expected to go to the sergeant, who would check with the commander. With less oversight, which lessened even more when the sergeant was replaced a few months later, the coding clerks were freer to make their own decisions. A slight change in how field reports were coded made a significant change in the official crime count. A change of two or three burglaries each day led to that 20 percent increase experienced in this southwestern city.

Finally, when the police department in the first southwestern city mentioned above instituted an experimental program for investigating all burglary complaints, official burglary counts dropped "abruptly" and rose abruptly when the experimental program ended. Normally burglary complaints were investigated by uniformed officers who wrote simple field reports when they responded to service calls. Detectives did not follow up with their own investigations if the field reports contained no leads, which typically they did not. Coding clerks then coded the field reports. During the experimental program, all burglary complaints were investigated by detectives, and clerks coded the crimes *after* the detectives investigated the complaints. These changes led to a decrease in officially counted burglaries. They did so for three reasons.

First, detectives have a better understanding of the complex *UCR* definition of burglary. For example, a building must be broken into and entered. An enclosed garage is a building; a carport is not. Breaking through a fence to steal something does not meet the *UCR* definition of burglary. When only uniformed officers investigated the complaints, some of their "mistakes" in classifying the crime were not "caught" by the coding clerks. Second, officers exercised discretion in classifying the crimes they investigated. For example, was the construction of a building far enough along for the crime to be a burglary or some other offense? Coding clerks were not always able to check the results of the discretion of the uniform officers. During the experimental program, the decisions of the detectives superseded the discretion of the officers. Finally, with all burglary complaints being investigated by detectives during the experimental period, double counting was minimized. Double counting could occur when a complainant realized that more items had been taken, called the police department to request that an officer be sent, but did not inform the officer that a previous complaint had already been made. The smaller number of detectives investigating the burglary complaints would more likely than uniform officers know if a previous complaint had been made (McCleary, Nienstedt, and Erven 1982). Organizational procedures are important in producing official counts of deviance.

CONCLUSION

Return to the opening question: how much deviance is there? I think that as much deviance exists as interested parties produce and use to meet their concerns. Through official and unofficial counts, interested parties produce the amount of deviance that exists. The counts do not present a "true" amount. Nevertheless, these counts can be useful.

If we know how they are created, then we can begin to decide how to use them. For example, if we know that official counts of school misbehavior are being produced in similar ways over time, then we can decide whether the misbehavior of students is changing over time. Perhaps school staff implement a new program to improve the relations among the children and between children and teachers. If the official counts of misbehavior then decrease, and if we have no reason to suspect that official counts are being produced in a different way, perhaps a way that would show a decrease even if students' behavior had not improved, then we can be confident that the new program is working. But we need to know how the counts are produced.

The next time you read or hear a report concerning the amount of some kind of deviance, or changes in that amount, question critically the report. Try to evaluate how the numbers were produced and for what purposes. Then decide how useful is the count.

PROJECT

1. Go to an agency that has official responsibility for handling deviance. Such agencies produce official information about deviance, perhaps including the amount of different kinds, the characteristics of the offenders, conditions of the offenses, and other information. Local and college law enforcement agencies, departments of mental health, child protection units of social service departments, school boards, or the offices of superintendents of education, and many other agencies produce official statistics of how much deviance has occurred.

Obtain the official statistic for some kind of deviance in which you are interested for a recent time period, probably the past year (or academic year). Talk with an official or staff member about how the official statistic is produced. What must officials within that agency do to produce an official statistic? For example, in order to have an official count of fighting within a school district, who must take what action that leads to an event being officially recorded as an instance of fighting? According to what you can learn, where in this process of constructing an official statistic are possible instances most likely not to be included? For example, do teachers report to their principals all instances of what they believe to be or suspect to be fighting? Do principals forward all such instances that come to their attention to the appropriate official in the district office? And so on. What may be some of the reasons for possible instances of deviance not being officially recorded? How are these official statistics used? By whom? How adequate are they for those purposes?

Can you think of a practical means for creating unofficial statistics about the deviance on which you focused? What may be some of the challenges of unofficially counting that deviance?

9

WHAT CAUSES PEOPLE TO
COMMIT DEVIANCE?

What causes people to rob, assault, cheat on their income taxes, defraud the government, murder, violate environmental regulations, fix corporate prices, and commit other deviance? If some of those acts of deviance seem distant from your world, then consider the following: What causes youths and young adults to cheat on their academic work, to drink underage, to use false IDs, to beat up others, to take drugs, to shoplift, to cheat their employers, to drink and drive, to vandalize buildings and homes (including mine), to engage in sexual activities as minors, and to commit other deviance? What do you think makes people act deviantly? Please take some time to write your response, then continue reading.

COMMON EXPLANATIONS

Many possible explanations for what causes people to commit deviance have been proposed. Some explanations focus on characteristics of individuals that cause the individuals to commit deviance. Other explanations focus on characteristics of the social conditions in which people live that make them engage in deviance. These two important approaches focus on *kinds of people* or *kinds of social conditions* (Cohen 1966, 41–47).

The individualistic, kinds-of-people explanations assert that defective characteristics of people cause them to commit deviance. Some people are seen to be *evil*. Their fundamentally

87

flawed selves, selves that embrace or are controlled by the "dark" forces of existence, are the root of their deviance. Traditional notions of being possessed by demonic spirits are the clearest expression of this explanation (Goode 1994, 70). More mundane examples are when people call those who act deviantly bad or no good. Others explain deviance by pointing to *psychological* defects of people. Mental illness, low self-esteem, a lack of self-control, or some other psychopathology causes deviance. Perhaps a sociopathic personality compels people to act deviantly. If not defective personalities, then perhaps some kind of *abnormal biology* is the cause of deviance. Some people may be born being more impulsive than others or less able to think through the consequences of their behavior. An abnormal biology may even be the basis for the psychological defects. Kinds-of-people explanations focus on various individual defects that cause people to commit deviance: evilness, psychological problems, biological abnormalities (Higgins and Butler 1982; Wilson and Herrnstein 1985; Katz 1988, Introduction; Collins 1992, 87–89).

Social scientists are more likely to propose that the social conditions within which people live or have lived may make them act deviantly. Some stress that *social strains* such as poverty, inequality, or an unhappy family may push people into deviance. Others emphasize that people *learn* to act deviantly through social influences. Family members, friends, and even the larger society, whether intentionally or not, shape people to act deviantly. For example, children who see their parents drink and use other drugs are molded differently from those whose parents abstain, even if the drug-using parents tell their children not to take drugs. The media may also provide deviant messages. Some social scientists focus on ineffective *controls* that fail to keep people from acting deviantly. Serious, certain, and swift punishment may keep people from committing deviance. Or the consistent concern of loved ones restrains people from acting unacceptably. Without these or other effective controls, people will act deviantly. These and other social scientific explanations emphasize inadequate social conditions that cause people to commit deviance (Higgins and Butler 1982, chap. 6).

Sometimes kinds-of-conditions and kinds-of-people explanations are combined to explain what causes people to commit deviance. People who grow up in "unhealthy" social conditions may become "defective" kinds-of-people who commit deviance. The social condition produces the individual defect that causes the person to act deviantly (Cohen 1966, 41–47). And still more explanations, which can become quite complex and may not be either pure kinds-of-people or kinds-of-conditions explanations, have been proposed to account for what causes people to commit deviance (Cullen 1984; Felson 1994; Gottfredson and Hirschi 1990; Link et al. 1989; Sampson and Laub 1993).

Look at your list of explanations for what causes people to commit acts of deviance. Do your explanations focus on individual defects, such as mental illness? Maybe you listed "destructive" motivations, such as greed, revenge, and the like? Did you propose unhealthy social environments, such as a "broken" family, peer pressure, the "deviant way of life" of a neighborhood, poverty or economic pressures? You probably listed a variety of explanations, though I imagine that many of them may have been stated as reasons why people act deviantly. Some may fit the various approaches I mentioned. Some perhaps do not.

I imagine that you may be wondering which of these explanations are correct. Maybe none is correct? Perhaps several of them are right? Or perhaps some in combination with one another are correct, as my students often tell me. I and others believe that *none* of these thoughtful explanations is *adequate*. Nevertheless, they can *become* quite useful if they are rethought. They are not at present adequate because they address a poorly stated question. The problem is the question that opened this discussion: what causes people to commit deviance? The simple answer for almost all deviance is that *nothing causes* people to commit deviance.

INADEQUACIES OF CAUSES

It is not helpful to search for the *causes* of deviance. None exist for most deviance that is committed—at least that is the argument of some social scientists. But that doesn't mean that we should not try to explain *how* people *come to commit* deviance. Some social scientists have developed intriguing ideas. I briefly mention one at the end of this discussion. Before reading my explanation of why no causes of deviance exist, try to think what arguments you might present to question the adequacy of causes to understand deviance, then continue.

By the concept *cause*, I think we generally mean a condition that produces an effect. For example, a lack of water caused the houseplant to die, the genes caused the individual's eye color, dropping the glass on the patio caused it to break, the virus caused the illness, and so on. But does any condition cause people to act deviantly? No, not for almost all deviance that is committed.[1]

Consider Jack Katz's (1988, 3–4) argument for abandoning the question: what causes people to commit deviance? Katz makes the following argument against the idea of causes. Many people who experience the proposed individual or social causes of deviance, such as particular hereditary characteristics or poverty, do not commit deviance. Others who do not experience those proposed causes do commit deviance. And still others who do experience those proposed causes sometimes commit deviance but for long periods of time do not commit deviance, even though they still experience the proposed causes. For example, at one moment, while being in poverty or having lived in a single-parent family, the person does not act deviantly, but at the next moment, still being in poverty or from a single-parent family, the person commits deviance. How can one argue that the poverty or living in the single-parent family caused the deviance? If you follow Katz's argument—and you may wish to reread this paragraph— then I think you will consider giving up looking for the *causes* of deviance.

You might object. I hope you do. You might object by responding that Katz's argument merely shows how difficult it is to discover the causes of deviance. Instead, you might argue that perhaps various conditions work in complex combinations under differing situations to cause people to act deviantly. Perhaps. But doesn't the possible objection stated in the previous sentence suggest that nothing makes people act deviantly? No condition, no matter how complex or subtle, determines that people commit deviance. Let's give up the concept of cause when thinking about how people come to commit deviance.

Instead, why not consider that, fundamentally, people move themselves to act, whether conventionally or deviantly. Nothing (typically) within or outside people compels, forces, dictates, makes, or causes them to do so (Higgins 1994, chap. 4). Nothing causes people to eat or not to eat, to go to work or to call in sick, to read a book or to watch television, to buy a car or to hold on to their present car another year, to study for a test or not to study, to yell at another person or to talk quietly, to come in from the rain or to get wet, to cheat on one's income tax or not, to assault another or to turn away, to drink and drive or to have a sober friend drive, to rob a store or not, and so on. Human behavior is not caused. Instead, humans behave.

People behave as they attempt to meet their concerns or their goals. When people experience a gap between their concerns and their present conditions, they may direct themselves to act to manage that gap. People may or may not be well aware of their concerns or of how they are directing themselves to act, but nothing causes people to act, not even their concerns.

People have many concerns or "desired states" toward which they move themselves to act. Some are physiological states, such as the biochemical balance of one's body, of which people are not consciously aware. Others are mundane concerns, such as having a meal to eat. Still others are deeply held goals. People develop most of their concerns as they live and act with one another. People can often move to meet their concerns in various ways. For example, one can eat different kinds of food in order not to experience being hungry. Or a student can take easy courses, study hard, cheat, or act in other ways in order to try to get acceptable grades in courses. People can even change their concerns in order to manage the gap. Disappointed in the progress being made in one career, a person may come to embrace another line of work as a goal. Or a student may come to decide that exploring new ideas and developing new skills are more important than getting certain grades in courses. Some concerns are more important to a person than are other concerns. The actions that people contemplate to meet their various concerns may clash. For example, people may be interested in developing successful careers through putting in long hours but also be interested in successfully raising families by giving their attention to their families. Those who commit deviance may initially experience a clash between maintaining an honorable self-image and the shame experienced in committing deviance.

People move themselves to act conventionally or deviantly. They do so without necessarily being able to explain to themselves satisfactorily how they came to act one way or the other this time. And even when they can explain satisfactorily to themselves how they came to act this time, we who are also interested in that issue may or may not decide that their explanations are adequate.

Thus, the question needs to be restated. Instead of asking the question, what causes people to commit deviance?, the better question is, how do people come to move themselves into deviance (and out of it)? Social scientists have developed explanations for that question (e.g., Douglas 1977; Higgins and Butler 1982, 179–200; Athens 1989; Pfuhl and Henry 1993, chap. 3). I do not think that any of these explanations are fully satisfactory, but they are promising.

SEDUCTION INTO DEVIANCE

Jack Katz (1988) has developed an intriguing approach for explaining how people move themselves into deviance. Let me summarize and illustrate it. I think that his approach is provocative, if also very unusual. To me, it is the best approach so far developed to explore how people move themselves to commit deviance.

Katz proposes that people *seduce* themselves into deviance. They create powerful feelings and understandings that at the moment seem to compel the people to act. It is as if the people could not have done otherwise, though they are the ones who created those compelling feelings. In doing so, however, they may not be well aware of how they did so. In fact, to be well aware of how they did so would be to make the feelings less compelling. Instead of being "caught up" in the moment and in the powerful feelings, those who were aware of producing those powerful feelings would be at least slightly "outside" of their self-seduction, looking at it.

People create these powerful feelings and understandings in response to challenges to their selves, as they understand and experience those challenges. Thus, *moral concerns*, concerns about who they are, not material concerns, concerns about what they have, are what matter most to people. These challenges to their selves arise out of the social worlds within which people make their lives. Thus, social conditions are important, but not as causes. Instead, they are important for the challenges that arise within them. Finally, those who seduce themselves into deviance must act, successfully managing the practical requirements for committing the deviance (Katz 1988, Introduction).

Sounds unusual, doesn't it? But consider the following. Have you ever become so mad, enraged even, at what another person said or did that you verbally assaulted that other person? Have you ever "worked yourself up" into an "uncontrollable" anger, making yourself madder and madder, perhaps as the other person continued to act in ways that you could not tolerate, screaming at the other person or heaping one criticism after another on that person? After you stopped, perhaps exhausted from your anger, you realized that you should not have done that, but it seemed as if you couldn't stop yourself during that rage. That rage may have lasted only a few seconds.

If you have had such an experience, try to recall it. If you can recall it, then do you remember powerful feelings and understandings that "gripped" you, ones that perhaps now you realize you created? Did these feelings and understandings concern maintaining your self-respect in the face of what you took to be the other's intolerable belittling of you? After calming yourself, did you wonder how you could have become so mad? Perhaps you were surprised at the ferocity of your anger. You did not realize that you could act that way. Or perhaps you realized that what the other did was nothing to become so enraged about. But at the time, you did enrage yourself.

RIGHTEOUS SLAUGHTER

The scenario I have just sketched, one that many of us have experienced in differing ways and degrees, is similar to Jack Katz's explanation of how people come to commit what he calls *righteous slaughter*. Righteous slaughter is an "impassioned attack" (Katz 1988, 18) in which the assailant reasserts his or her honor by violently attacking the one who dishonored him or her. The violence of the attack attests to the depth of the dishonor that was done.

For example, a wife whose husband abuses her and flauntingly cheats on her may come to feel that her fundamental self-worth is being stripped from her. Being abused once again and/or catching her husband in yet another episode of infidelity, one that he does not deny but rubs her face in by boasting how good he and the other woman were together, the wife may experience profoundly degrading humiliation. She cannot imagine how she can go on like this. She may then transform this humiliation into rage through a sense of righteousness that blinds her to any future consequences. Through a violent attack on the husband, perhaps accompanied by shouting and cursing, the wife attempts to obliterate the degradation and the one who degraded her. Whether the husband dies or not, the fury of the attack reasserts the wife's dignity—at least for the moment. The fury of the righteous slaughter attests to the wife's worthiness that the husband had defiled.

The husband's abuse and degrading infidelity did not cause the wife to feel humiliated. Her humiliation did not make her enraged. Her righteous rage did not force her to attack her husband violently. *Through* these powerful feelings and understandings created by the wife, she moved herself into deviance. She did so in a way that for the moment may have seemed beyond her control.

While more investigation is needed, righteous slaughter appears most likely to be committed by those with relatively few resources, those who are poor or "working class." Their worlds may provide many, even continuing, occasions to be humiliated. Work may be demeaning, and intimate relations may be peppered with disrespect. Those with few resources may have few options for managing their humiliation successfully. When those with more resources are humiliated, they may be able to retreat to private offices, escape from hell at home by going to work or taking business trips, immerse themselves in civic activities, buy the consumer appearance of respect, and so on. If righteous slaughter is done in defense of one's moral worth, then under what social conditions are people's moral worth most likely challenged and when are those people so challenged likely to have relatively few possibilities or capabilities for successfully managing that humiliation? Yet the social conditions do not cause the slaughter. Instead, profound challenges to the self may be experienced within those social conditions.

SNEAKY THRILLS

Different instances of deviance may involve different moral concerns, different challenges to people's selves, different emotions and understandings, and different practical requirements for successfully committing the deviance. For example, committing righteous slaughter is not the same as committing shoplifting, stealing a car for joyriding, sneaking underage into a bar, vandalizing a neighbor's house, or committing other *sneaky thrills*. Let me briefly present this second example, sneaky thrills, a kind of deviance perhaps more familiar to you.

Have you ever committed a sneaky thrill? Many, perhaps most, of us have done so. Try to remember what you did and your experience. The example I give concerns a teenage female's shoplifting. Males shoplift too, but Katz's investigation of sneaky thrills primarily concerned women.

A teenage female goes shopping. She may or may not have gone with the intent to "take" something. As she browses in a store, a bracelet "catches" her attention. It seems to call to her. She cannot take her eyes off it. She has to have it. Even though she has the money to pay for it, it would be so easy to take it. The "taking" of the bracelet gives it an appeal that as a mere object it does not have. But what if she is caught? She would "just die."

The teen moves back and forth between the excitement of taking the bracelet and the horrifying thought of getting caught. Her ambivalence and oscillation increase the attractiveness of the object, of the deviant project she is contemplating. The excitement and tension increase. The lure of the object, of the deviant taking, grows stronger. The teen begins to act out the thrilling larceny in her heart while concentrating on maintaining a conventional appearance. But how should she act like a shopper when her desires are anything but honorable? What she previously did with ease as an honest shopper now becomes a challenge to manage as her intent has turned deviant.

The young woman may produce one or several emotions. She may experience a thrill of courting danger but also the presence of mind and control to overcome it; the excitement of exploring and committing what could be profoundly humiliating without others sensing her deviant desires; the exhilaration of competing against the "other" (i.e., the store and perhaps particular store personnel) and winning; the rush, perhaps almost a sexual rush, as the tension of the deviant action builds and then is released with its success; the satisfaction of asserting one's self against the constraints of conventionality; the euphoric realization that her self contains more possibilities than she imagined, but without committing herself to a deviant future. It was just playful. All of these and more emotions make sneaky thrills profoundly moving.

The teen may never use the bracelet or may throw it away. She may vow never again to do such a "crazy" thing. She may feel ashamed for what she did or not. The store may forever be transformed, no longer just a place to shop, but now having a magical quality of where she pulled "it" off. The sneaky thrill may be remembered and emotionally reexperienced for years, perhaps even a lifetime. I can still recall decades later some of my sneaky thrills.

While adults engage in sneaky thrills, youths may find sneaky thrills particularly appealing, enabling them to manage challenges to their selves. Youths are often self-conscious. Everyone seems to be watching them. What do those observers see? Do the youths measure up? They may feel that they do not and wonder how easily others can see that. Can others notice their inner inadequacies and their devious desires? Are their private selves publicly visible? How well can they manage the appearance of their selves? If their inner selves are easily seen, then what they can do, what they can get away with, becomes greatly curtailed. Sneaky thrills enable youths to test their capacities for presenting and concealing their selves, for being devious and getting away with it. Sneaky thrills provide opportunities for discovering the possibilities of their selves in a "playful" way that does not commit themselves to a "truly" deviant path (Katz 1988, chap. 2).

Consider your deviance. Did you move yourself into deviance to meet your concerns? How did you seduce yourself into deviance? For example, what understandings and emotions did you create for yourself if you cheated academically, bought alcoholic beverages illegally, stole from your employer, beat up someone, or sped "wildly" over the speed limit? The emotions may not have been as charged as those involved in righteous slaughter or as euphoric as those involved in sneaky thrills, but perhaps they were adequately compelling to enable you to commit deviance *at that moment* when you did not do so the previous moment. To what challenges to your self was your deviance a response? Did anything *cause* you to act deviantly? I don't think so. What do you think?

LINKING SEDUCTIONS, SOCIAL CONDITIONS, AND KINDS OF PEOPLE

We may not be satisfied with Katz's intriguing approach. But his approach provides us with one way of beginning to make sense of how people come to commit deviance when nothing causes them to do so. It does not ignore the social conditions that some social scientists present as the causes of deviance. Instead, it begins to link those social conditions to the challenges to their selves that people experience, to the moral challenges to which deviance may be a response. Thus, righteous slaughter becomes linked to the humiliation of poverty or working-class existence; sneaky thrills to the concern with the contours of one's self experienced in adolescence.

While Katz does not make the connections, we can even begin to see links between kinds-of people explanations for what causes people to commit deviance and his approach that explores how people move themselves into deviance. For example, people with lower self-esteem or with lessened biological capacity to control themselves may more easily or quickly seduce themselves into some kinds of powerful feelings and understandings than may others.

Nevertheless, we should not take the example I just presented to mean that Katz believes that seducing oneself into deviance is a sign of being defective. Not at all. Self-seduction is a very creative act, one that can explore and expand the possibilities of oneself, as in sneaky thrills. Yet self-seduction can be creatively destructive, as in righteous slaughter.

We may also be able to combine kinds-of-people and kinds-of-conditions explanations and link them to Katz's self-seduction approach. For example, the social conditions of people's lives may have been a catalyst for the people to develop different capacities and orientations, which then enable the people to more or less easily seduce themselves into deviance.

The creation of dangerous violent criminals, who ruthlessly attack others, may be understood in this way. Out of social conditions of brutalization, those who become dangerous violent criminals may become belligerent, resolving to attack others physically who provoke them. They resolve not to be again violently humiliated. With success in attacking those they understood to be disrespectfully provoking them and with the admiration and fear of others, those who become dangerous violent persons embrace their resolve to use violence, even against those who do not provoke them unduly. They become malevolent, brutalizing others as they once had been brutalized. But they conjure up the powerful feelings and understandings of malevolence *at a particular moment*—and, through those compelling feelings and understandings, they move themselves to attack another violently at *that* moment (Athens 1989).

CONCLUSION

Through Jack Katz's approach, we can begin to think about the causes of deviance in a different, more useful way. We will not abandon the common kinds-of-people or the kinds-of-conditions explanations. Instead, we will transform the kinds-of-people approach into capacities and orientations with which people manage the challenges to their selves. The kinds-of-conditions explanations point to differing social conditions people experience and out of which challenges to their selves may arise. As people move to meet their concerns, they possess various capacities and encounter differing challenges.

To return to the question that opened this discussion, what causes people to commit deviance? the simple answer is nothing. But from my discussion of that simple answer and my presentation of one alternative—Katz's examination of seduction into deviance—I hope you realize that how people come to commit deviance is not simple at all. What do you think?

NOTES

1. Conditions that are deemed deviant may be caused by genes, hormones, diseases, and other conditions that directly affect the body. Disabilities, which are often reacted to negatively, including mental illness, may be caused by various conditions that affect the functioning of the body. Certainly drug use can impair or alter the body's functioning, which then may be implicated in deviant acts that the impaired person commits, such as vehicular homicide. But, typically, nothing causes people to commit deviance.

PROJECTS

1. Ask individuals what they believe causes people to commit deviance. Compile a list of responses. Try to categorize those responses as kinds-of-people explanations that emphasize traits and characteristics of people or kinds-of-situations explanations that emphasize social conditions that propel people into deviance. Are you unable to classify some of the explanations as either one or the other type? If you wish, you could ask individuals to tell you what they think are the top three (or five or whatever number you wish to use) causes of deviance. Are kinds-of-people explanations emphasized more or less than kinds-of-situations explanations? Can you categorize the kinds-of-people explanations into different types? the kinds-of-situations explanations into different types? For example, maybe some of the kinds-of-people explanations stress biological defects; others emphasize psychological difficulties. What types of these two explanations are most given? What other insights do you develop from this project?

2. By examining your commission of deviance (or a friend's), investigate the compelling emotions you created, your understandings of how others viewed you, and the practical requirements you managed as you moved yourself into deviance. To what moral challenges to yourself do you think your deviance and its compelling emotions were a response? This may be difficult to do. To analyze the magical qualities of seducing oneself into deviance requires one to distance oneself partially from the magical moment in order to reflect on it. The magic then loses some of its spell; the deviance may be aborted. Yet, if the deviance was accomplished, then one may have been caught up in the deviance to such an extent that one cannot usefully report on what one was thinking, feeling, and doing when committing the deviance. Friends may try to explain why they committed the deviance instead of what they thought, felt, and did during the deviance episode. Good luck.

10

HOW DOES MEANING MATTER IN COMMITTING DEVIANCE?

Have you ever been mugged? Has someone you know been mugged? What happened? Recall if you can, then continue.

Perhaps something similar to the following happened. A stranger, typically a young male, comes upon you. The young male may ask you for the time or a dime or directions, then he tells you to "give it up." He may flash a weapon or intimate that he has one. Or the young male may grab your purse and run. Some may grab, push, or hit you when they take your wallet, purse, watch, or other valuables.

Muggings can be terrifying experiences. While those who are victimized realize that muggings occur, perhaps even often in their communities, they typically are not expecting to be mugged. They carry out their everyday activities with some comfort and ease. They are unprepared for what befalls them. Their safety is threatened; their property is taken. They become chillingly vulnerable. Those who are mugged may come to mistrust their world. Places and people become suspect. They may alter their routines in order to guard against future victimizations. They may do so to the extent of imprisoning themselves in their homes. If they did not resist, they may be angry, even ashamed. Their world and their place in the world may not be the same for a long time afterward (LeJeune and Alex 1973).

Now, consider muggings from the stance of the muggers. What may be key for a successful mugging? Please think about that and write your response. When you finish, then continue.

I imagine that you may have mentioned physical prowess, fearlessness, size, willingness to hurt others, or some other attribute of those who mug as crucial for mugging successfully. Perhaps you mentioned catching the victim off guard and unprepared or having a weapon in order to be in charge. All those things can be important in mugging. But *meanings* are crucial, too. How participants interpret the situation is important in muggings.

MEANINGFUL MUGGINGS

Successful muggings, successful at least to the muggers, depend on the meanings that participants produce. In fact, meanings matter in deviance of all kinds, as I will illustrate briefly with other kinds of deviance after discussing muggings.

Consider the person who mugs. While citizens may fearfully imagine muggings—being ripped off by a stranger in which harm may be done—those who mug, especially novices, may be afraid and uncertain. Those who mug confront a risky, uncertain situation. They do not know whether they will succeed or whether they, not the victim, will be harmed. Citizens, after all, may carry weapons or forcefully resist. Those who mug confront the challenge of creating meanings for themselves and for the victims such that they (1) satisfactorily reduce the fear and risk that they experience and (2) gain and maintain control over their victims so that the victims cooperate in the muggings.

Those who mug, especially novices, are often scared. They don't know what may happen to *them*. Will they pull it off? Will they be caught? Will the victim resist? Does the victim have a weapon? Will they, the muggers, be hurt? Those who mug develop meanings to reduce that fear. Early successes embolden those who mug. Muggings come to be seen as less risky. Initial muggings may be done in a group. Comrades give heart to one another as they hide their fear from one another behind a shaky bravado. Afterward, they recount their exploits, reliving close calls, bragging about what they did, congratulating themselves on their successes. Some may use drugs to control their fears. Others may never control their fears well.

Those who mug are concerned about the police, witnesses, and victims. All pose a risk to them. Victims are especially important, as those who mug confront them directly. Selecting victims can lead to favorable meanings for muggings. If you were to mug, on what personal features would you focus in picking a victim? Consider this question before you continue.

You may likely wish to mug someone you believe will not resist much and will have something worthwhile to take. Those who mug may use these two commonsense principles—or at least say they do when they talk about their muggings. But those who mug are likely to do so when "on the stroll," when walking through areas with which they are familiar and in which they will not be obtrusive. For inner-city males this means inner-city areas. Therefore, while they may wish to mug those who seem to pose little risk and have valuables to make it worth their while, whoever is available may be the ones they rob.

When those who mug confront potential victims, their challenge is to get and maintain control of the victims and of what is being done. The muggers attempt to catch the victims off guard so that the victims cannot prepare to defend themselves or flee. Thus, those who mug may dress conventionally, in ways that do not fit the stereotypes that people have of criminals. They may unthreateningly or less threateningly approach victims, asking for directions, cigarettes, or loose change. But the muggers also must make clear their intentions. They must define to the victims that this is a mugging, that they are serious and capable, and that the victims should "willingly" participate in their own muggings.

It may seem easy to define clearly to the potential victims that they are about to be mugged. "Give me your purse" is clear. But that may not be so. Victims are not expecting to be mugged, even though they may know well that muggings are not infrequent. Being caught off guard, they may not quickly realize what is taking place. Ironically, the practices of muggers to catch their victims off guard may make it more difficult for them to define quickly and successfully that they are mugging the victims. Thus, potential victims may smile, joke, wonder if the muggers are kidding, express surprised disbelief, or in other ways not immediately define the action as muggings.

When potential victims do not quickly realize that they are being mugged, then those who mug must make extra efforts to define for the victims what is about to happen and the victims' role in it. Muggers may repeat that this is a "stick-up" or "rip-off." They may flash weapons or forcefully claim that they are serious. They may grab or push the victims in order to make clear that what is about to happen is no joke.

Those who mug need to control the potential victims in order to mug successfully. They do so by showing that they are tough and/or by using physical force. Mugging in a group, brandishing a weapon, playing on the fears that many citizens have of young black men, talking and appearing tough, and other practices may enable those who mug to make clear to their victims that they should cooperate. Some muggers use physical force or weapons to show that they mean business. Inexperienced muggers may hit victims or grab victims in order to get control without first telling the victims that they are being mugged. Some may react to what they perceive as the victim's resistance by using force, by hitting the screaming victim or the victim who claims to have no money. Through a posture of toughness and/or the use of force, muggers attempt to define clearly to the victims the seriousness of what is happening and to direct the victims in the role they are to play in their muggings.

This brief sketch, based on the work of Robert LeJeune (1977), shows the importance of meanings for muggings. Those who mug and those who are mugged create meanings and have meanings presented to them that matter in the muggings. Muggers are most successful when they create meanings that enable them to reduce their fear and uncertainty, define clearly for the victims what is occurring, and gain and maintain control over the victims.

Meanings matter in committing deviance more generally, not just for muggings. Now, consider homicide and domestic violence. While my examples all concern coercive deviance, deviance in which offenders use force or threaten to use force against victims, meaning matters for any kind of deviance (Best and Luckenbill 1994).

HONOR IN HOMICIDE

Consider homicide that is not done in the commission of a robbery or other crime. Consider the killing between family members, friends, acquaintances, co-workers. One way of making sense of such murders is to see them as "character contests" (Luckenbill 1977). In the character contest the murderer and/or the murdered are trying to establish, save, or regain "face" (i.e., one's dignity) at the expense of the other as each stands up to the other's disrespect. If the adversaries do not back down, neither one apologizing for the disrespect that the other experienced, then they may escalate the character contest to murder. Other participants at the confrontation—friends, colleagues, onlookers—may supply meanings to the character contestants that, if acted on by the contestants, escalate or lessen the confrontation.

For example, two friends may be driving in a car. One tells the other that while his parents are great people, he is a leech, who is always sponging off his parents. The one called a leech could back down and, in effect, accept that verbal slap to his face. Or he might yell at or curse the friend who acted disrespectfully toward him. The friend could apologize, which would likely end the contest at that time. Or the friend may continue to put down the one he called a leech. If others are in the car, they may try to cool down the combatants or perhaps intentionally or inadvertently "egg" them on, potentially escalating the seriousness of the character contest. If neither contestant backs down, then they may create the mutual understanding that violence will be used. The outcome of that mutual understanding may be murder.

This example may seem trivial, but it is based on an actual murder (Luckenbill 1977). Respect and disrespect are crucial for many homicides. Even if some character contests seem to be about meaningless matters, meaning does matter in murder.

INTERPRETATIONS IN WOMAN BATTERING

Consider domestic violence, specifically woman battering. Millions of women experience violence in their marriages and intimate

relationships. You might expect that after the first episode of violence, women would leave their husbands or mates. But they do
not. They typically endure more violence, sometimes for months
or years. They are not masochistic, enjoying the battering. Instead, they deal with complex and confusing emotions, understandings, opportunities or the lack thereof to make their lives
without the abusers, and other features of their situations. They
may have great feelings for the men who batter them. After all,
the men are their husbands, mates, or intimate friends. They may
have children they may be uncertain they can support without
their husbands or mates. They may wonder whether the battering
is temporary. They may wonder what the men will do if they do
leave. These and other considerations make battering relationships complex.

Battered women typically stay for a while in the battering
relationship. They do so in part through interpretations that they
create and use. These interpretations make the battering less serious, perhaps absolve the men of some of the responsibility for
the violence, and in other ways lessen the urgency to do something drastic about the battering, such as leave the batterers.
These interpretations give a very different meaning to the events
than you and I, looking from the outside, might give to them (Ferraro and Johnson 1983).

For example, women who are battered may claim that their
husbands or mates batter them because of alcoholism, work pressure, or some other external force, not with an intent to harm the
women. Further, the women need to save their mates, to help them
get over the difficulties that push them to batter. Some interpret the
harm they suffer as tolerable, or they give little attention to it, focusing on the bulk of their time with their mates that is satisfactory.
Others define themselves as somewhat responsible for being
beaten; perhaps they should not have nagged their mates to the
point where the mates battered them. Some believe that they have
few options. Where will they go? How will they support themselves and their children? A battered relationship is better than
none, they reason. Acting upon meanings supplied by their society,
others believe it is their duty as wives or their religious duty to
support their men. Outsiders may supply meanings that make it

difficult for battered women to define their situations as intolerable. In-laws may not provide a sympathetic ear or actively discourage women from interpreting the events as intolerable violence. All of these and more interpretations enable women to remain in battering relationships long after the first act of violence.

But interpretations can be changed. Battered women may create new meanings that serve as a catalyst for them to leave the battering relationship—at least for the moment (Ferraro and Johnson 1983). With a change in the level of violence, perhaps from the use of fists to pulling the trigger of what turns out to be an unloaded gun, battered women may reinterpret their relationships and leave. As options become available, such as a shelter for battered women, the battered women may redefine their future as one in which they can succeed without their mates. Or, if the mates' remorse decreases and the women experience long periods devoid of affection, they may come to believe that they must make a dramatic change. Family members, friends, or others may help the women to redefine their relationships as intolerable and encourage them to do something about it. Shelter workers may impress on the battered women who reluctantly or ambivalently consider leaving their mates the seriousness of the situation (Loseke 1992). Through the meanings supplied by others, the women may redefine their relationships and leave. And when they create future meanings, such as becoming weary of their abusive mates' persistence in locating them, extracting promises from their mates not to abuse them again, or making their children who may remain with their mates their first priority, they may return to their abusers (Baker 1997).

The "violent" acts of the mates do not themselves produce the meanings held by the women. As the women deal with their complex, confusing relationships and situations, they create and use meanings that matter greatly.

CONCLUSION

Force is an important feature of muggings, homicides, domestic violence, and other coercive deviance. But force is not the only crucial component of coercive deviance. It is not even the most important component. The meanings that the participants create for themselves and for one another are crucial in committing deviance.

While I have focused on coercive deviance, meanings are important for all deviance. I urge you to explore how meanings that participants produce for one another are important in doing drugs, cheating—both academic and on one's mate—employee deviance, shoplifting, police graft, corporate crime, and on and on. For example, have you purchased an alcoholic drink when underage or know people who have done so? If so, then you know that those who are underage manipulate how they appear so that those who check identifications believe they are of legal age. Underage drinkers try to create false meanings. How they do so can be quite ingenious. Deviance does not "just happen." Instead, offenders, victims, and others *meaningfully* commit deviance.

PROJECTS

1. Offenders and others involved in deviance produce meanings—interpretations and feelings—that enable deviance to be committed. One form of interpretations is called techniques of neutralization (Sykes and Matza, 1957). These are interpretations that those who commit deviance use to lessen the sting of the negative reactions from others who would condemn them, including themselves. These techniques of neutralization can be understood as after-the-fact justifications. They can also be understood as interpretations that enable offenders to lessen the offensiveness of what they are doing as they contemplate doing the activity, in doing the activity, and afterward in anticipation of future deviant actions. Offenders may deny that they are responsible for what they did; deny that any harm was done; deny that the so-called victim was actually a victim, but, instead, was someone who got what was coming, asked for it, enjoyed it, or in other ways was not victimized; criticize those who condemn the offender for being hypocritical about their own faults and shortcomings; and/or appeal to being loyal to friends or upholding some other virtue.

Talk with people who have committed deviance—cheating, underage drinking, illegal drug use, shoplifting, or other offenses. Explore with them how they understood their deviance. Perhaps ask them if they thought what they did was wrong (or terribly wrong) in order to encourage them to think about how they understand their deviance. What, if any, kinds of techniques of neutralization do they use?

2. Ask these same people to explain how they came to commit deviance at the time and place that they did. Why had they not done it earlier or at another nearby place? These questions will invite the people to explain their reasoning, their meanings, that moved them into deviance at that moment. Don't force the people to provide responses if they have difficulty answering, however. They may not have thought much about their deviance at the time they did it or afterward. And even if they can provide responses to your questions, you should wonder whether that is how the people understood their actions at the time of the deviance, not days or weeks later in talking to you.

11

WHAT HAPPENED?

Was it shoplifting? Did sexual assault occur? Was the killing murder? Sometimes, what happened seems obvious. At other times, it is not at all clear what took place. Whether obvious or not, what happened may be a more complex matter than we realize. How what happened comes to exist and who is "responsible" for what it is that happened may be surprising. Let me present three different events. All occurred. As you read each event, please write what happened.

THREE INSTANCES OF DEVIANCE—MAYBE

First, I recount an incident I witnessed when out with my family. One Saturday night, my wife, our two daughters, and I went to a family-style restaurant. We waited behind a waist-high railing as we moved toward the counter to obtain our silverware and plates and order our meal. Behind us arrived a family: father, mother, and their son, who appeared to be about five years old. (Actually, I assumed the people were a family. I did not ask them.)

The young boy stood on the lowest rung of the railing, which was a few inches off the ground. His dad called to him to rejoin the family. When the boy did not do as his father commanded, the dad repeated his order. The boy did not comply. The father took hold of one of his son's arms and pulled the boy toward him, away from and off the railing. A moment later, the boy slipped free of his father's grasp and returned to the railing. The father then hit his son hard in the boy's back with the knuckles of his closed hand. The son cried loudly.

Now, what happened? Reread my account if you wish, then formulate your response. I'll return to this event after presenting two other incidents.

This second event occurred a few years ago in Austin, Texas. The account is based on newspaper articles. On September 16, a twenty-five-year-old woman returned home from a party a little before 3 A.M. The leatherwork artist undressed and went to bed. Awakened by her barking dog, she turned on a light and confronted twenty-seven-year-old Joel Valdez, armed with a knife. The woman locked herself in her bathroom and began to call 911. Valdez broke down the door, knocked the phone out of the woman's hand, assaulted the woman, and ordered her to take off his pants. The woman thought that he was going to kill her. According to both the woman and Valdez, he told the woman not to worry, he did not have AIDS. The woman replied, "How do you know I don't?" Valdex answered that he didn't have any condoms. The woman gave him one. Valdez then had sex with the woman for almost one hour before she escaped from him, ran from her house without clothes on, and summoned help from a neighbor.

Valdez was arrested the next day and charged with aggravated sexual assault. According to a police report, Valdez admitted that he entered the woman's house, "held a knife to her and had sex with her." But he denied that he raped her. "There was no rape to it," he said. "She's the one gave me them condoms. She's the one took my pants off and put it on me. She told me to put the knife down and I did. After that, she started telling me about AIDS, then reached into her purse and put on the condom" (Milloy 1992, Garcia 1992). What happened?

One final incident. This occurred in a school in my city. Again, it is based on newspaper accounts. On a winter's day a few years ago, a high school student, James Dunbar (names have been changed), fought with friends of another high school student, Frank Black. Black was not involved in the fight. Nevertheless, Dunbar blamed the fight on Black and slapped him in the face. Conflicting testimony was presented that Dunbar also pulled

a gun on Black and threatened to kill him. Dunbar had been expelled the year before for bringing a gun to school. Testimony
was presented that Dunbar was a "violent troublemaker." That
night Black got a gun, test-firing it to make sure it worked.

The next day at school, Dunbar approached Black in the
crowded hallway of their school as students changed classes. According to Black, Dunbar aggressively crossed the hall toward
him, not stopping even after Black pulled out his gun. Though the
unarmed Dunbar did not try to strike Black, nor did Black see
Dunbar with a gun, Black began shooting Dunbar when Dunbar
was a few feet away. Black shot Dunbar four times. Disputed testimony was given that Dunbar was shot in the back (Greene
1995). What happened? Make your response, then continue.

Let's return to the first event in which the father struck his
son. What do you think happened? When I ask students what
happened, they respond in various ways. Some reply that a father
disciplined or punished his misbehaving child. Others say that the
father punished his son in an inappropriate way. Still others answer that what occurred was child abuse.

I do not know what "really" happened. Yet I was as much an
eyewitness as anyone in the restaurant. I was not more than a few
feet from the incident. I was troubled at whatever happened. My
wife and I briefly talked about it while eating. But I did not do
anything about it. I did not say anything to the father. Most observers who believe that an adult has gone "too far" in punishing
a child do not confront the adult. If they do, they may be challenged by the confronted adult, who believes the matter is not
their business (Davis 1991).

Later, I telephoned the county office of my state's department of social services and talked to a social worker within the
child protection unit of the agency. The social worker told me that
under state law "abnormal" punishment is child abuse. What I
witnessed could be abnormal punishment; hence, it could be child
abuse. But what I witnessed was not child abuse. How do I
know? Let me explain after revisiting the other two incidents.

Recall the second incident that occurred in Austin, Texas, in
which a knife-wielding intruder had sex with a woman after the
woman put a condom on the man. What do you think happened?

The intruder obviously sexually assaulted the woman. Rape is what happened, according to my students who are presented with the information. The grand jury hearing the case voted *not* to indict the man for sexual assault. Although grand jury proceeding's are secret and no reason was given, one participant reported that some jurors believed that the woman's protecting herself by putting a condom on the intruder may have implied her consent. An assistant district attorney thought that the grand jury simply made a "mistake." It had heard 550 cases over three months and had already considered 30 cases the day it decided not to indict Valdez. A month later, another grand jury hearing the case did indict the intruder on charges of aggravated sexual assault and burglary with intent to commit sexual assault. (*New York Times* 1992, Phillips and Garcia 1992). So, what really happened? Based on what I have presented so far, we do not know what happened. Let me explain after returning to the third incident.

In the third incident a student shot an unarmed student four times in a crowded school hallway, killing the young man. What do you think happened? The jury returned a verdict of *not* guilty of either murder or the lesser charge of voluntary manslaughter. What happened was not a criminal homicide. More than one and one-half years after it occurred, the killing became what it was. How can that be? Let's explore the three incidents for insights about the occurrence of deviance.

TRANSFORMING EXPERIENCES INTO WHAT HAPPENED

A father strikes his child, a knife-wielding intruder has sex with a woman who puts a condom on him, a teen shoots and kills an unarmed student. These three events do not announce to us what they are. No labels come attached to tell us whether the father's striking his child is abuse, whether the knife-wielding intruder's sex with the woman is rape, whether the killing of the unarmed student is a criminal homicide.

People classify their experiences of these three incidents as one or another kind of event. Experiences may be direct, indirect, or a mixture of both. I had direct experiences through observing the father striking his son. You had indirect experiences from reading my account of my experiences. Both grand juries in the alleged case of sexual assault in Austin, Texas, had indirect experiences of the incident. You and I had experiences that were even more indirect than the grand juries' experiences, experiences based on newspaper accounts and my reports of the newspaper accounts. The jury that found the teenage student not guilty of criminal homicide had indirect experiences of the incident. Once again, you and I had experiences even more indirect than the jury's experiences. People do not transform the incidents into one or another kind of deviance or nondeviance. They transform *their experiences* into what happened.

To know what happened—to understand whether a specific instance of this or that kind of deviance occurred—we must explore the transformation of people's experiences into what happened. The following are some of the issues we might examine in that transformation. We may be interested in learning *who* is involved in that transformation. Participants, witnesses, officials of various sorts, and still others may be involved in transforming their experiences of incidents into what happened. For example, in order for the incident in Austin, Texas, to become a sexual assault, the woman, police, prosecutors, a grand jury, and eventually a jury (if the case went to trial, which it did, ending in a guilty verdict (Phillips 1993)) would have to transform their experiences into rape.

But don't think that all instances of deviance involve officials transforming their experiences of events into what happened. The examples I have presented did involve officials in various ways. But much deviance does not. Family members, friends, colleagues, and other ordinary citizens are often the only ones who confront the challenge of deciding what happened in any particular case. And when officials are involved, they become involved typically only after ordinary citizens have transformed their experiences into instances of deviance and then reported "what happened" to officials.

We might explore *how* the various participants transform their experiences. For example, what understandings do participants use in transforming their experiences? Perhaps some members of the first grand jury reviewing the incident in Austin, Texas, made the assumption that by supplying the intruder with a condom, the woman was giving her consent to the sex. Members of the second grand jury apparently did not make that assumption.

Or consider an assumption made by prosecutors in one West Coast jurisdiction when handling alleged sexual assaults. They may become suspicious of apparent inconsistencies in the claims of women who report being sexually assaulted. A woman typically tells her story to several criminal justice officials. If prosecutors notice differences between the versions that they cannot account for as a result of the woman's being confused or upset after the assault, then the prosecutors may not believe the woman. Or, if the woman's account of what happened does not fit the prosecutor's knowledge and experiences of such cases, then prosecutors may also question the credibility of the woman (Frohmann 1991).

For example, a deputy district attorney questioned the credibility of one victim's allegations because of what the deputy district attorney took to be inconsistencies between the victim's account given to police and the account given to her. In the police report the victim stated that all three men involved in the incident kissed her. In the interview with the prosecutor the victim said that this was not so. The prosecutor also wondered about the inconsistency between the police report that stated that the victim and the assailant sat on the couch and watched television when they reached the assailant's room and the victim's interview statement to the prosecutor that she was forced into the assailant's bedroom immediately after arriving at his room. The deputy district attorney thought that the differences in the police report and the statements made by the victim to her were "strange because there are things wrong on major events like oral copulation and intercourse." The prosecutor assumed that the police are not going to make such mistakes in writing a report and that these discrepancies involve "major events" about which a victim would not make mistakes (Frohmann 1991, 216). The prosecutor then questioned the credibility of the victim.

The *context* within which the participants transform their experiences may be important to us. For example, what concerns do the participants face? When the West Coast prosecutors mentioned above evaluate a sexual assault claim, they know that conviction rates are used by their superior to assess their competence. A pattern of not-guilty verdicts points to the incompetence of prosecutors. That pattern also points to prosecutors' lack of commitment to the "organizational concern of reducing the case load of an already overcrowded court system." Finally, judges may question the competence of prosecutors if they continually pursue cases that, according to their outcomes in court, should have been rejected (Frohmann 1991, 215). Within this organizational emphasis on convictability, prosecutors transform their experiences of women's allegations of sexual assault into what happened.

Part of the context within which people transform their experiences may be the larger cultural understandings of what constitutes this or that kind of deviance. For example, people's beliefs about what constitutes sexual assault have changed greatly in the past several decades. When more than 200 women, eighteen years or older, living in a southern town, were surveyed more than twenty years ago, 19 percent said that the following event was rape: A woman and man who have been dating for three months are at the man's apartment. After kissing and embracing for some period of time, the woman tells the man that she wants to stop. The man continues and "after a struggle, he has sexual relations" with the woman. Twenty-one percent thought that possibly rape had occurred. Sixteen percent were uncertain. Twenty-three percent thought that rape probably had not occurred. Twenty-one percent thought that it had not occurred (Klemmack and Klemmack 1976, 139). When I have asked my students to ask their friends, almost all say that rape has occurred. And still other issues in how people transform experiences into what happened will concern us.

CREATING WHAT HAPPENED

I believe that my discussion leads to the probably uncomfortable conclusion that we can never know what "really" happened. My discussion leads even a little further. Not only can we never know what really happened, but what happened does not exist independent of what people claim happened. People create what happened as they classify their experiences as this or that kind of deviance or nondeviance. They may do so easily; they may do so with great difficulty. They may do so with consensus or with great disagreement. To the extent that people do so easily and with widespread agreement, then they are more likely to believe that they have truly recognized what happened. That certainty is comforting. That certainty is also important for people to be able to live and act with one another. But it is a certainty that masks the responsibility of those involved for transforming their experiences into what happened.

No matter how certain people are, they cannot check their claims of what happened against what the event "really" is. They can check their claims against others' claims. They can use commonsensical assumptions, such as assumptions about who is likely telling the truth, for deciding the adequacy of their conclusions about what happened. They can use very sophisticated procedures for deciding what happened. But the event is not anything until people transform their experiences into what happened.

Do not misunderstand me. I am not saying that "nothing" happened when the first grand jury did not indict the knife-wielding intruder. I am not saying that the woman did not experience an event that terrified her and harmed her. After all, we have her report to that effect—and to an extent, the intruder's report, too. But that event was transformed by many people in various ways. It did not become officially a sexual assault until the defendant was convicted eight months after the incident occurred.

Did the first grand jury make a "mistake"? Yes, but the first grand jury did not make a mistake because the event was "really" a sexual assault. The first grand jury made a mistake only after the second grand jury and the trial jury had officially classified the event as a sexual assault. Once classified, that is what happened—for all official purposes. I imagine that most of us would agree that the event should be classified as a sexual assault.

CONCLUSION

Now you should be able to explain my conclusion to the three in-cidents with which I began this discussion. How do I know that when I witnessed a father's hitting his son, I did not see child abuse? After the second grand jury indicted the Austin intruder on a sexual assault charge, how could it still not be known what hap-pened? How did the killing of the student in a crowded school hall become a legal killing, not a criminal homicide, more than one and one-half years after it occurred? How would you now re-spond to those three statements?

My responses are: The father did not abuse his son when he struck him. He did not do so because my state department of so-cial services did not transform that incident into an instance of child abuse. Except when I called the county office of the agency and spoke to a professional hypothetically about that incident, the agency had no experiences of that incident. They had nothing to transform into child abuse. The father did hit his son and likely hurt him. I thought what the father did was wrong. But it never became an (official) instance of child abuse.

When the second grand jury indicted the intruder for sexual assault, that incident had yet to be officially transformed into a rape or something else. An indictment is a legal accusation, not a finding of guilt. As it happened, the defendant was found guilty of rape and faced a sentence of up to life in prison. At the mo-ment of guilt, the incident became rape, at least officially so.

The killing of the unarmed student did not become what it now is—a legally defensible homicide—until more than one and one-half years after the teenager's death. Events can become in-stances of one or another kind of deviance or nondeviance only *after* they occur, not when they occur. The future always decides what happened in the past. To think about what happened is to explore how people in the future transform events of the past.

Thus, you, I, and all others who transform their experiences are "responsible" for what it is that happened. We are not respon-sible for the actions of the parties involved. But we—as family members, colleagues, officials, teachers, administrators, and in many other capacities—are responsible for transforming our experiences of events into what those events become. We produce what it is that happened. It can be a troubling responsibility if we think about it. But no matter how troubling, it is a responsibility that we cannot escape.

PROJECT

1. What happened in deviance is produced through the interpretations and actions of those concerned with what occurred. Participants, observers, and others who learn of an event may decide what happened. Officials who become involved always construct what happened. They must in order to do their job.

Observe the proceedings of traffic court, criminal court, or some other board that decides what occurred concerning some alleged deviance. Colleges have various boards that decide whether students, faculty, or other members of the college have violated college policy. Those boards are likely to proceed in secrecy, however; the public is not admitted. Many cases of what happened will not be contested in traffic court and criminal court. Traffic violators will not contest their citations; offenders will plead guilty. The important work of constructing what happened has already occurred before the case is disposed of in court.

But you will be able to observe some of the construction of what happened during trials or hearings. Criminal trials may take longer than you are able to observe. Traffic cases are likely to be concluded more quickly. Examine how the opposing parties try to construct what happened. What arguments do they present? What information do they present to support their claims of what happened? How do they, if they do, try to discredit the presentation of the opposing party as to what happened? If you are able to talk with any of those involved in the court cases, you might try to explore what they did to prepare for court, to prepare for constructing what happened.

12

WHAT KIND OF PERSON IS THE OFFENDER?

When a person commits deviance, family members, friends, colleagues, officials, and others may try to learn why the person committed the deviance. In exploring that question, the family members, friends, and others will likely try to discover what kind of person is the offender. Is the offender primarily a conventional individual who happened to commit deviance? For example, in a moment of panic and under great pressure, a "good" kid may cheat on a test without having planned to do so. Or, is the individual a deviant kind of person, this offense being a result of the individual's unacceptable character? An unemployed highschool dropout may commit a robbery of a convenience store, the latest in a string of robberies, muggings, and thefts. Who is the offender? This issue may be more puzzling than first imagined.

WHO IS SUSAN SMITH?

Consider the following nationally publicized case. A twenty-three-year-old mother strapped her two sons, three years old and fourteen months old, into their car seats, drove to a nearby lake, and rolled the car into a lake. The boys drowned. For nine days, she claimed to law enforcement officials and to the nation that a black man carjacked her car with her two boys in the back seat. She pleaded for the man to return her sons. As law enforcement officials investigated and began to suspect that she had killed her sons, the young mother confessed to what she had done.

120

This tragedy occurred in my state, South Carolina. What kind of person is this young woman, Susan Smith? What kind of person must Susan Smith be to kill her two sons and then lie to a nation for more than a week? What do you think? Please consider this question carefully, write your response, then continue.

Let me tell you more about Susan Smith. Accusing her husband of being unfaithful, Susan Smith sued him for divorce three years after they married. Accusing Susan of adultery, her husband later countersued. During this marital strife, she became involved with the "most eligible" bachelor in town, the handsome son of a wealthy businessman, in whose company Susan worked. They lunched together, and they went to be alone to the house she and her estranged husband had bought as newlyweds.

The man was apparently not as serious about their relationship as was Susan Smith, however. Seven days before Smith drowned her sons, she received a "Dear Jane" letter from him. He wrote that he was ending the relationship with her because, among other reasons, he was not ready to assume the responsibility of raising her young sons. Susan Smith ran into her ex-lover at a restaurant the day before she killed her sons. The ex-lover, sitting with some women during happy hour, sent Susan a beer. A few minutes later, she left upset, according to bartenders. The next morning, the day that she drowned her sons, she approached her ex-lover and told him that she had had an affair with his father while both were in New York on business. Later that morning, she told her ex-lover that she had made up the story of the affair with his father. That night, Susan Smith drove eight miles to a deserted lake into which she rolled her car with her sons strapped in their car seats, drowning them.

What do you think now? Is Susan Smith horribly evil, willing to kill her sons in order to regain the attention of her wealthy boyfriend? Please take a look at what you first wrote about Susan Smith, write what you now believe, then continue.

Let me tell you some more about Susan Smith. When Susan Smith was six years old, her parents divorced. Her mother won custody of Susan and Susan's two older brothers. The following month, her father, taking the breakup with his highschool sweetheart hard, killed himself with a shotgun blast. Susan was told that her father was happy and in heaven. From then on, she wanted to join her father in heaven according to expert testimony at her trial.

The next year, Susan's mother married a prominent businessman in town, and Susan and her family moved to one of the nicer neighborhoods in the city. Her life seemed to go well until she took an overdose of aspirin when she was thirteen. When she was sixteen, she told her mother and sheriff's deputies that her stepfather repeatedly molested her for months. He would often come into her bedroom late at night and molest her. One time, after being molested for six months, she asked her stepfather to hand her a towel while she was in the bathroom. He then spied on her while she was in the shower. According to a Department of Social Service file, her stepfather later admitted to sexually assaulting Susan. Both were ordered to undergo counseling, and the stepfather was ordered to move out of the house. Susan and her mother did not press criminal charges. A year and a half later, when eighteen, Susan overdosed again on aspirin. She was hospitalized for eight days for depression and adjustment disorder.

Sixteen months later and two months pregnant, Susan married her husband. The marriage was turbulent. Her husband admitted cheating on Susan and striking her at least twice. They had terrible fights, according to Susan's husband. He once chased her into their yard and tackled her. She became disinterested in having sex with him. Tight money created discord. Susan left her husband when their older son was five months old; later she returned. He left her when their younger son was two or three weeks old.

Susan was involved in several destructive sexual relationships. The incestuous relationship with her stepfather, begun in her adolescence, continued into Susan's marriage. The last time was two months before the death of her sons. When she was eighteen, she was involved with two male co-workers, forty and thirty years old. She attempted suicide when she thought she was pregnant from one of those relationships. She continued to have sex with her estranged husband. She was also involved with the wealthy father of her lover, the "most eligible bachelor" in town. She became depressed when her estranged husband threatened to tell the wealthy man's wife that her husband, old enough to be Susan's grandfather, was involved with her. When Susan Smith confessed to killing her sons, she stated that she planned to kill herself, too, but backed out (Decker 1995; O'Shea, LeBlanc, and Decker 1995a, 1995b, 1995c).

Now what do you think? What kind of person is Susan Smith? Is she a profoundly troubled woman, who has been abused and used by older men? Is she the perpetrator of a horrible deed, but not horribly evil herself? Or is Susan Smith a truly wicked person, who calculatingly killed her children in order to further her desires?

Does it matter who Susan Smith is? Does it matter whether she is a deeply emotionally disturbed woman who killed her two sons, whom she loved, as she grappled with her lifelong troubles and with more immediate crises? Does it matter whether she is a manipulative, highly skilled deceiver who put her desire for rekindling the affection of her wealthy lover above the lives of her children? Certainly it mattered to the prosecution and the defense attorneys. It mattered to the jury. The kind of person Susan Smith is was important in the jury's deliberations to sentence her to life in prison or to death.

Who is Susan Smith? The prosecutors portrayed her to be a conniving woman who tried to improve her social position by drowning her sons in order to regain the affection of her wealthy ex-lover. The defense attorney presented Susan Smith as a deeply, mentally troubled woman, whose emotional problems grew from the time her father committed suicide. The tragedy she created grew out of her tragic life. The jury came to know Susan Smith to be a severely depressed, disturbed individual, who had an "irrational" way of seeing things according to one juror. She needed help for her "mental illness," according to another juror. She knew what she was doing when she killed her sons, but she was emotionally troubled, not horribly evil. Hence, the jury unanimously voted on its first ballot to sentence her to life in prison (Warren and LeBlanc 1995).

The kind of person the offender is, is crucial for the phenomenon of deviance. When officials and others grapple with what to do to the offender, they consider the offender's identity

(Higgins and Butler 1982: chaps. 4 and 5). Officials and others do not react only to the offense. They react also to the offender. If the offender was acting under duress, is truly remorseful for the offense, has led a fine life, or in other ways is generally conventional, then officials and others react less harshly toward the offender. But if the offender freely chose to commit the deviance, does not care about the harm caused, has a history of deviant behavior, or in other ways is generally offensive, then officials and others react more harshly toward the offender. Who the offender is matters greatly, as it did in the trial of Susan Smith.

But who is this offender, Susan Smith? What kind of person is she? Do you think the jury was right, that Susan Smith is a profoundly emotionally troubled woman who needed help? Or was the jury wrong? Is Susan Smith primarily a manipulative, deceptive person who chose to involve herself in unhealthy relationships and who killed her sons in order to enrich her life? *How can we know?*

CONSTRUCTING THE OFFENDER'S IDENTITY

We cannot know what kind of person Susan Smith "really" is. We cannot know what kind of person any offender really is. Instead, we *construct* the identities of offenders. But we typically do not realize the great responsibility we have for who others "are" (Higgins 1994, chap. 3).

Instead, we likely believe that we are trying to discover who the offender is. We assume that the offender is a certain kind of person, with a definite set of traits. Our attempt to discover that identity may be difficult. It may be difficult to sort out conflicting information and to judge the genuineness of statements by or about the offender. It may be difficult to evaluate the impact of life events on the offender. The offender may be complex. Our attempt to discover who the offender is may not be fully successful. But we assume that we are looking for an identity that exists within the offender.

Consider a different approach to the question, who is the offender? The offender is who we make the person to be. We—

officials, jury members, family members, friends, colleagues, and others—give an identity to the offender. We do so as we piece together the information we have concerning that person. We piece it together within a social context of assumptions about what people are like, of relations we have with the offender and with other parties involved in the issue, of concerns that we are trying to manage.

It is not possible to discover the identity of the offender or of anyone. Instead, we have experiences "of" the offender. We may have personal involvement with the offender and/or we may learn about the offender through what others present to us. We have experiences of what the offender did and said and our reactions to that. We fashion an identity for the offender out of our experiences.

Even our experiences of what the offender did and said are not pure representations of what the offender "really" did and said. People can witness the "same" event but see what happened quite differently. People can hear the "same" testimony but understand what was said very differently. What the offender did and said must also be constructed. Recall the previous chapter, "What Happened?"

We cannot compare the identity we constructed for the offender to the offender's "true" self. We cannot do so because no true self exists independent of people constructing selves for others—and for themselves! Just as we construct identities for the offender, the offender constructs an identity for herself or himself. At best, we can compare the identity we constructed to other experiences we have concerning the offender—future experiences, new information, what others now present to us, and so on.

We may be able to decide whether the identity we attribute to the offender is useful for our purposes. For example, a parole board decides that an inmate has reformed himself (most inmates are men) and is interested in making a law-abiding life for himself. The board paroles the offender. The parole board members can then evaluate somewhat the identity they gave to the inmate, with how he does when paroled. If the inmate succeeds on parole and afterward, then the parole board members will be confident that the identity they gave to the inmate served their purposes well. If the inmate violates parole through committing new crimes and is returned to prison, then the parole board members may question greatly the identity they gave to the inmate and how they came to give that identity to him. They may decide to change how they assess inmates who come up for parole review.

But the construction of an identity for an offender cannot be true. It cannot be false, either. To be true or false would imply that we can know the actual identity of the offender and then can judge the accuracy of our construction. That is not possible.

Instead, we should ask other questions concerning the identity of the offender. For example, who is interested in constructing an identity for the offender? Why are these people interested? For example, what are their relations to the offender? What are their goals in constructing an identity for the offender? What resources are available to them for doing so? How are they doing so? For example, how are they selecting some information, not other information; how are they interpreting the information; what assumptions are they using? How useful is the identity constructed of the offender for the people who constructed the identity? For example, does the identity construction enable the constructors to meet their concerns well? *To understand who is an offender, we need to explore how people construct the offender's identity.*

The construction of the offender's identity is quite evident when parties contest the identity of the offender. Accusers and defenders may create starkly contrasting identities for the offender (Emerson 1969). They did so in the trial of Susan Smith. They also did so in the trial of another young woman in my state, whose child died a year before the tragedy of Susan Smith and her two sons.

CONTESTING IDENTITIES

Mary Alesia Sonnier was sentenced to five years in prison after pleading guilty to unlawful neglect in the death of her three-year-old daughter. The battering of the baby led to her being brought by ambulance to a local hospital where she remained on life support for twenty-nine months until she died. The prosecuting attorney portrayed the young woman to the judge as a neglectful mother who allowed her child to be battered worse than any child had been battered that the prosecutor had seen. The prosecutor could not understand how a mother could have allowed her child to be so badly battered—to have her ribs broken in fifteen places, her arm broken, both shin bones bruised, her leg broken, her head and abdomen beaten, and her thumbs bruised and swollen. The baby was unresponsive to most stimuli during her twenty-nine months on life support, which was "evidence of the most extreme degree of brain damage," according to the prosecutor.

Mary Sonnier's attorney depicted her as a strikingly different person. The young mother was a child herself, dominated by a "boyfriend" twenty-seven years older than she. The high school student dropped out of the eleventh grade when pregnant and was sent to Texas by her family to have her baby. While in Texas, she was called for several months by Donald Kelley, who was known by Mary's mother. After the birth of her baby, Sonnier's mother brought Mary back to Columbia and "effectively" into the hands of Donald Kelley, said the attorney. Kelley was married but also lived with a "number of women," the attorney said. The attorney claimed that Mary Sonnier was Kelley's "doll, his toy." Kelley was "insanely jealous." He abused Sonnier, "beating her in the head with a pistol until she lost sight in one eye." The attorney implied that Kelley had been the one who abused the baby, not Sonnier. Instead, Sonier was a "victim, and she was a child." After Kelley's death from a heart attack, Sonnier had "turned her life around." She lived in an apartment and worked as a computer operator. While I do not know what identity the judge gave to Mary Sonnier, the judge sentenced Mary Sonnier to five years in prison, half of the maximum sentence (Zupan 1994).

CONCLUSION

Constructing the identity of the offender occurs often during the dramas of deviance. Whenever people manage the offender, they are constructing an identity of that offender. They decide what kind of person this offender is and how they should handle the offender. Teachers construct identities for their misbehaving students; law enforcement officers do so for those they confront; mental health professionals predict if someone is dangerous or not; juries may try to decide whether the accused is the kind of person who could commit the offense; judges consider the remorse of the convicted offender in passing sentence; parents wonder about the character of their children who have acted unacceptably; and so on.

Who, then, is Susan Smith? Like any offender, Susan Smith is whoever the involved parties have created her to be. That is an awesome responsibility, which most of us are not willing to recognize as ours. But whether or not we recognize that responsibility, we cannot avoid it. When you are involved in the dramas of deviance, encountering those who have committed deviance, consider carefully how you and others construct identities for the offenders.

PROJECTS

1. We do not uncover the identity of the offender. We construct it. Participants may clash in their construction of the offender's identity. You can witness how participants construct the identity of the offender and the clash between detractors and defenders by observing the sentencing phase of criminal court cases (or other disciplinary hearings). During that phase, prosecutors will likely try to convince the judge or jury that the offender deserves a particular sentence because of the heinous nature of the offense *and* the offender. The defense lawyer is likely to present the offender as a less offensive kind of person, one deserving of more understanding or compassion. How do opposing attorneys construct the identity of the offender? What strategies and reasoning do they use? What information, such as character witnesses, do they present? If you are able to talk with the attorneys, then you may be able to explore how the attorneys prepared for this important production—the production of the offender. If you can talk with whoever decided the punishment, you can examine how the decision maker(s) made sense of the identities presented and what identity the decision maker(s) fashioned of the offender.

2. Newspapers may construct an identity for an offender in well-publicized, nonroutine cases. In trying to present to the public who the accused (and perhaps later convicted) is, newspapers will investigate the past and present of the accused and present what they have "found." But they do not present what they have found as unconnected bits and pieces of information. Instead, they connect the bits of pieces into an identity for the offender. They may present opposing interpretations (i.e., identity constructions) of supporters and detractors. They may present inconsistencies. But they will likely attempt to present a coherent portrayal of the offender. And if not, they will present the conflicting portrayals that others provide. Examine how they do so.

3. If a group to which you belong is dealing with a member who is considered to be acting inappropriately, explore how the other group members identify the offender. Do group members give the offensive member a deviant identity? Do other members give the offensive member a more conventional identity? If so, then how do those members explain why the offensive member is acting inappropriately? Do members who disagree about the offender's identity try to persuade one another or try to convince undecided members of the offender's identity? Can you make any sense of why some members give the offender a more deviant identity than others? For example, are those who give a deviant identity to the offender not close in their relation to the offender? What else can you explore about this identity construction?

13

IMAGES OF HARM OR HARMFUL IMAGES?

To start with, I ask you to think quickly, without reflection, then write your response to two questions. After you read the first question, quickly write your response. When you finish, then read the second question and quickly write your response. After writing both of your responses, then continue reading. Are you ready?

> *First question*: When you think of crime, what specific crimes come to mind? Quickly list them.
> *Second question*: When you think of a criminal, what visual image of the criminal comes to mind? Quickly describe that visual image as well as you can.

When I ask my students to respond to these two questions or to have their friends respond to them, the responses typically have much in common. Maybe your responses are similar to theirs.

When you thought of crime, did you respond, as my students and their friends typically do, by listing murder, robbery, assault, rape, burglary, drug addiction, and other "street offenses"? Did you list corporate fraud, embezzlement, political corruption, violations of securities laws (e.g., insider trading of stocks and other manipulations of stocks, bonds, and other financial products), workplace safety violations, price fixing, and other "suite offenses"? My students do not typically mention these suite offenses done by seemingly respectable people within mainstream companies and organizations.

When you pictured a criminal, did you describe, as my students and their friends typically do, a male, perhaps young, likely low income, maybe scruffy or tough looking? Did you give the criminal an ethnic or racial identity as a minority citizen? I know that issue is particularly sensitive. Or did you picture a woman, someone dressed in a business suit, an executive, government official, or professional? I imagine that you likely did not. Few of my students or their friends do so.

THE TYPICAL CRIME AND THE TYPICAL CRIMINAL

Instead, many of us have acquired an image of the Typical Crime and the Typical Criminal (Reiman 1995, chap. 2). When we think of crime, we usually think of predatory offenses done intentionally by one or a small number of offenders against one or a small number of victims. These could be called street offenses, though they are not just done "on the street." When we think of a criminal, we usually imagine a young male who is tough looking, perhaps even a minority male. We are much less likely to think of illegal behavior that indirectly victimizes people done by those who are seen as respectable members of the community. These might be called suite offenses to distinguish them from those that typically come to mind.

Research on the stereotypes that people have concerning crime and criminals supports Jeffrey Reiman's argument and the results I have obtained from hundreds of students. For example, Thomas Gabor (1994, chap. 2) asked graduate students in criminology to select the two men out of a choice of six men they thought were most likely to have committed an armed robbery. None of the men pictured had committed an armed robbery. The students overwhelmingly selected among three men who "looked" the toughest or scruffiest—one had long hair, another had a clean-shaven head with a dangling earring, and the third looked like a young Fidel Castro. Gabor also asked the students to select the two men who were least likely to have committed armed robbery. Again, the students overwhelmingly selected among the other three men who "looked" to be the mildest.

Another investigator found that when asked to select photographs of people most likely to have committed armed robbery or murder, individuals typically selected pictures of people's faces that had been consistently rated as unattractive by a previous panel of raters (mentioned in Gabor 1994: 29-30). Much other research indicates that people have facial, social-class, and ethnic/racial stereotypes of who is a criminal. This research supports well Jeffrey Reiman's notion of the Typical Crime and the Typical Criminal.

Jeffrey Reiman and others argue that our images of crime— the Typical Crime and the Typical Criminal—are displayed to us by the media. When politicians talk tough on crime and campaign for votes, they, too, focus on the Typical Crime and Criminal. Some of you might object. The Typical Crime and Typical Criminal are not figments of your imagination or illusions presented by the media and politicians. Instead, you might argue that most crimes are street offenses done by low-income, often minority males. Certainly millions of street offenses are reported to the police each year. Poor minority males are more likely to commit such offenses than are those with other social characteristics, though scholars debate this issue. Certainly many individuals who are not poor minority males commit such offenses, and most who are poor minority males are not high-rate offenders (Elliott and Ageton 1980; Reiman 1995).

While a basis exists for the Typical Crime and Typical Criminal images, those images may greatly mislead us. They may mislead us in many ways. I discuss two ways. First, the Typical Crime and Typical Criminal images encourage us to view crime as done by a certain segment of citizens, a segment with fewer resources and respect. These images overlook that crime is widespread. Recall chapter 2, "Who Is Deviant?" People from "all walks of life" commit crime. Most people have committed behaviors that clearly fit the legal definitions of crime, even if they have never been caught or punished (Gabor 1994). Have you drunk when under age, tried an illegal drug, stolen something from a store, taken an item from an employer, cheated on your income taxes, assaulted (hit) someone, or committed other crimes? Probably so. While most people have committed crimes, most do not regularly commit serious offenses. Nevertheless, the Typical Crime and Typical Criminal images mislead us to think crime is committed by a certain segment of people, not by a wide range of people.

Typical Crime and Typical Criminal images mislead us in another, related way. These two images tell us that we have most to fear from those who are least successful in society. These images encourage us to look "below" us when we are worried about our safety, not to the "side" or "above" us in society. Would you be surprised to learn that most harm to people and to their property is done by executives, managers, professionals, white-collar workers, and other successful people (Reiman 1995)?

Americans have more money stolen from them through white-collar offenses than by street criminals. Approximately $200 billion is stolen in America each year through consumer fraud, embezzlement, pricefixing, securities fraud, bribery, tax fraud, and other white-collar offenses (Reiman 1995, 109–12). This is almost 6,000 times the amount that bank robbers got away with in 1991 and more than eleven times the amount stolen in all thefts reported in the FBI's *Uniform Crime Report* for 1991 (Reiman 1995, 111). We know we have been victimized when our car stereo is stolen or we are mugged. Suite offenders pick our pockets without our typically realizing it.

More people die or are physically harmed each year through the hazards of their work than are murdered or assaulted. For example, in the early 1990s approximately 24,000 people were killed annually through murder or nonnegligent manslaughter. Approximately 1 million aggravated assaults occurred, according to law enforcement. During that same time period, a conservatively estimated 35,000 deaths occurred yearly as a result of occupational hazards, and almost 2 million work-related disabling injuries or serious job-related illnesses occurred annually. Much of this occupational harm and many of the deaths reflect the failures of management to provide safety features and government to enforce safety standards (Reiman 1995, 70). While occupational and criminal harms are underreported, occupational harms may be more likely underreported than criminal harms (Reiman 1995, 70-74). Further, only about half the American population works; whereas all citizens are at risk of being a victim of crime. Therefore, the figures for crime need to be halved or those for occupational harms doubled in order to compare the *likelihood* of citizens being harmed by street offenders or suite offenders.

HOW TYPICAL IMAGES ARE CREATED

According to Jeffrey Reiman (1995), the criminal justice system operates so that it helps to produce and maintain a "visible" class of criminals, the Typical Criminals who commit Typical Crimes. How does it do so? It does so by not dealing with known sources of crime, by primarily focusing on only some of the harm that people commit, and by not enforcing the law as vigorously against those who are successful in society as against those who are not successful.

First, society and the justice system do not seriously address what are some of the important sources of street crime: the impoverishment of hope and opportunity that many low-income people experience; the failures of prisons to reform; the widespread availability of guns; and a misguided war against drugs. This war against drugs increases the cost to obtain the drugs, which increases the likelihood that users and addicts may steal and rob to obtain the money to buy the drugs, the profit to be made in selling the illegal drugs and the use of violence to protect the illegal businesses and profits. Not all scholars agree with Reiman's assertion of these sources of crime. You might look at chapter 9, "What Causes People to Commit Deviance?"

Next, by focusing primarily on one-on-one street harms, such as murder, robbery, and assault, rather than on indirect harms, such as occupational hazards, chemical assaults on citizens (through pollution, food additives, and even smoking), and unnecessary and dangerous medical practices, society narrowly defines what is crime or what is serious crime. It does not proclaim that these indirect harms are serious enough to use the full force of the state to control them.

Third, by more likely arresting, prosecuting, and imprisoning poor minority offenders than white-collar, professional, and corporate offenders, the criminal justice system fills society's prisons with only some of the people who harm Americans. Have you ever visited a prison? I encourage you to do so. But do not be misled. The typically poor minority men that you will see there are only a portion of those who harm their fellow citizens. Through these three processes, the criminal justice system creates a visible class of criminals who, indeed, typically have harmed others.

Typical Crime and Typical Criminal images help protect the advantaged position of those who are successful (to varying degrees) in America. First, when concerned about their safety and their property, most people fear those who are unsuccessful. Citizens, politicians, and other officials do not give comparable attention to the harm done by those who are successful. When politicians talk tough about crime, they are talking about street crime, not harm from the suites. The harmful practices of executives, professionals, white-collar workers, and other (relatively) successful people who enrich themselves may go uncontrolled.

Second, the unequal opportunities for becoming successful in society are not seriously addressed, either. When the typical criminal is found guilty, the criminal's individual responsibility is stressed. Society is let go. Social conditions, such as the impoverishment of hope and opportunity that many poor people experience and that may be mitigating circumstances, are judged not to be important. Further, as the typical criminal is responsible for his crime, so is he seen as responsible for his poverty. He and others like him are viewed as part of the dangerous class. They are a danger to the safety and well-being of America and its moral citizens. Unequal opportunities, such as the great inequality in schooling and job opportunities (Wilson 1996), are downplayed as sources of crime and poverty. Finally, those who have the greatest capacity to change the justice system, those who are well off, have little reason to do so. They, too, accept the images of the Typical Crime and the Typical Criminal and benefit from those images being widely held (Reiman 1995, chap. 4).

Most who are successful do not routinely, seriously harm their fellow citizens, just as most who are low income do not do so either. Many in the criminal justice system are dedicated and compassionate. Yet people with good intentions can create or help maintain harmful arrangements.

IS THE JUSTICE SYSTEM CRIMINAL?

To end this discussion, let me raise the following question posed by Jeffrey Reiman: Is the criminal justice system just or is it criminal? That may seem like a harsh question. Yet, is every system of law just? Do you believe that the legal systems in Nazi Germany, the former Soviet Union, South Africa when it embraced apartheid, China, and other countries are or were just? Was the American legal system just when it promoted slavery and then discrimination?

The criminal justice system and crime both use force. They may even use deadly force. Criminals use force to coerce people to act against their own interests and for the interests of the criminals. The criminal justice system presumably uses force to coerce some people to act in order to protect the interests of all in freedom and security. To be superior to crime, the justice system must use force fairly applied to all who harm in order to protect all equally. To the extent that it does not, then the criminal justice system is less just and more criminal (Reiman 1995, Conclusion). The creation, use, and consequences of the images of the Typical Crime and the Typical Criminal indicate that the criminal justice system at present falls short of being a system of justice.

To conclude, do our images of crime and criminals capture well the harm to which we are exposed? If not, are those images harmful to a more useful understanding of how our well-being is threatened? What do you think?

PROJECTS

1. Ask a sample of friends or fellow students to list quickly what crimes come to mind when they think of crime. Give people perhaps thirty seconds. Ask them or another sample of people to describe quickly what image comes to mind when they think of a criminal. They should include any physical description that comes to mind. Compile the list of crimes. Examine the images of the criminal. Do these fit the notions of The Typical Crime and The Typical Criminal of which Jeffrey Reiman writes? Do any contradict these notions? Do some responses point, instead, to suite deviance, such as corporate fraud committed by successful citizens?

2. Examine a sample of issues of a newspaper. (You might try to examine a sample over a month or a year instead of over a few days in order to have a more representative sample of what the newspaper typically presents.) Identify all articles about crime. What crime(s) is(are) the focus of each article? If pictures of the defendants are presented, note their race, sex, and, if possible, their (probable) social status. Such information may be included in the articles. Compile this information. For example, what percentage of articles discuss typical street crimes; what percentage discuss corporate, professional, and other suite offenses? Recall, street crimes, such as murder, can be committed by professional people. What percentage of the pictures present minority and/or lower-status offenders? What percentage present European Americans and/or middle- or higher-status offenders? What do you conclude are the images that newspapers present about harm and who commits it?

3. You can explore other media, such as television or movies, for the images they present of crime and deviance. Use the directions for project 2 to guide you.

14

WHO COULD CAUSE SUCH HARM?

What kind of people would knowingly, physically harm others? What kind of people would cause others such harm that those harmed would scream in pain, would cry out not to be harmed? What do you think? Please write your response, then continue.

Perhaps you wrote that disturbed, emotionally troubled, or evil people would act so cruelly. Maybe those with mental health problems or who had been seriously abused as children might commit such harm. Such people might be sadistic, enjoying the torment of others. Let's explore this issue further by examining some well-known research.

THAT'S SHOCKING

Imagine that you are asked to participate in research concerning memory and learning conducted by a professor at your campus. You will be given about $5 as thanks for your participation. Do you think you might be willing to participate, especially if it took only about one hour?

If you do, when you arrive at the designated place for the research, you are greeted by the professor. The professor explains to you and another volunteer that he, the professor, is interested in the effects of punishment on learning. To explore those effects, one of the volunteers will be the learner; the other volunteer will be the teacher. Any time the learner makes a mistake in the learning activity, the teacher will electrically shock the learner. With each mistake of the learner, the teacher will be expected to

138

increase the intensity of the shock by 15 volts to a maximum of 450 volts. The levels of shock are labeled with terms such as "slight," "moderate," "strong," and even "XXX." While the shocks can be "extremely painful," they produce no "permanent tissue damage," says the professor. Through the luck of the draw, you are selected to be the teacher; the other volunteer will be the learner. The professor shows the equipment to you and the other volunteer and provides a sample shock to you (labeled 45 volts on the shock generator) so that you know how it feels.

Would you now participate? Would you shock the other volunteer when that person made a mistake? If so, how far would you go in shocking that other person? Would you throw the switch 30 times, going to the maximum shock, 450 volts? Please write your response and your reasoning, then continue.

I imagine that you responded that you would not shock the learner to the highest level when the person made a mistake. Perhaps you were willing to shock the learner mildly, but then stop after a few shocks. That is what college students, psychiatrists, and middle-class adults told Stanley Milgram (1974), the Yale professor who conducted this well-known research. Everyone he asked replied that they would not shock the learner to 450 volts. They would stop well before that level. The vast majority, 90 percent, responded that they would stop before level 13, 195 volts, labeled "very strong shock." They also believed that most people would stop well before the highest level of shock. Only a tiny percentage of people, less than 1 or 2 percent, would shock the learner to the highest level, thought these adults.

Most of us are decent, caring people. We would not harm others by shocking them, certainly not for making a memory mistake. Disturbed people would harm others, not decent people. Thus, the responses of the psychiatrists, college students, and middle-class adults should not surprise us. They are decent people, and they know that most people are decent.

Indeed, Milgram encountered difficulties in doing his research. In developing the specific procedures for his research, he struggled to create a procedure in which *every* teacher did *not* continue to the highest level of shock! Almost every volunteer shocked to the highest level when the learner was placed in a room separate from the teacher and the learner did not protest the shocks. Mild protests from the learner were also inadequate. Milgram eventually strengthened the protests to include references to a heart problem, repeated shouts to be let out, and agonized screams.

By the way, while ethical criticisms were made of Milgram's work, the learner was not actually shocked, though the teacher did not know that during the research. The learner was a confederate of Milgram who posed as another volunteer. Through a rigged draw, the confederate was selected to be the learner.

Milgram conducted many versions of his research. The learner typically sat in a room separate from the teacher, but in some versions the learner was in the same room as the teacher. The researcher usually sat in the room with the teacher, directing and prodding the teacher to continue with the research if the teacher hesitated to continue. In one version, the researcher left the room after giving the initial instructions to the teacher and by telephone continued to direct and prod the teacher to continue. In another version, the research was done at an office in Bridgeport, Connecticut, not at Yale University, where most of the research took place. In still another version, the researcher was unexpectedly called from the room before explaining what shock levels to use when mistakes were made by the learner. While gone, a third volunteer (actually Milgram's confederate), who was to record times from a clock at the researcher's desk, "got" the idea that the teacher should increase the shock level each time the learner made a mistake. Throughout the experiment, this apparent volunteer insisted that his suggestion be followed. In one version, the teacher chose the level of shock to administer. Milgram developed still more versions of his experiment (Milgram 1974).

The percentage of teachers who shocked to the highest level varied among the different versions of the research. For example, when the learner was placed in a room separate from the teacher, groaned, screamed in agony, and pleaded to be let out, with his protests tied to particular shock levels, and with no more responses to the questions at 315 volts, 63 percent of the teachers went to the highest level of shock. When the learner was placed in the same room as the teacher, 40 percent went to the highest level. "Only" 30 percent went to the highest level when the learner was in the same room as the teacher and the teacher had to place the learner's hand on a shock plate at the 150-volt level or beyond, because the learner would not put his hand on the plate. When the teacher chose the level of shock, 3 percent chose the highest level. And so on (Milgram 1974).

What do you think about this research? What might it suggest to us about deviance? Please write your response, then continue. I believe Milgram's work suggests several insights about deviance, insights that question our common sense about deviance.

ORDINARY DEVIANTS

Many of us view deviants as dramatically different from ordinary people. We take for granted that those who commit deviance, especially serious deviance, are different kinds of people than we are (Goode 1978, chap. 5). We couldn't do that. For example, we couldn't seriously harm others. Milgram's work challenges this common sense. Instead, humans have great capacity to harm others as well as to help others. If people can make harming others compellingly understandable and felt—reasonable, sensible, necessary, unavoidable, deserved by the others, "no big deal," a duty to be carried out, and so on—then they can harm others.

People may make harming others compellingly understandable and felt in many ways. I do not explore the variety of ways in which it is done. In chapter 9, I explored how people create powerful feelings and understandings that enable them, compel them, to commit righteous slaughter (Katz 1988, chap.1). Lonnie Athens (1989) explores how people come to be dangerous, violent persons with a (horrific?) willingness to harm others violently. But people also harm others in more ordinary situations. For example, most parents hit (i.e., use corporal punishment on) their children, which often hurts them (Straus 1991, 1994).

The volunteers who became the teachers in Milgram's research were ordinary people. Recall that in one version of Milgram's research, the teachers chose what shock level to administer. Just one out of forty volunteers chose the highest level.

Thirty-eight of the forty volunteers chose a level no higher than 150 volts, level 10. These forty volunteers resembled the volunteers who participated in the other versions of Milgram's research. These were ordinary people who had no pathological desire to harm others.

A diverse group of ordinary people participated in Milgram's research. These ordinary people varied in their experiences, background, personalities, and in other ways. It did not take a certain kind of person to inflict apparently agonizing harm on the learner. For example, it was not "weak willed" people or "brutal" people who shocked the learner.

With the "help" of Milgram and his assistants, who played various parts in the research, the ordinary citizens made shocking the learner compellingly doable. From the moment they responded to the advertisement to participate in the research, they created a willingness, even an obligation, to continue what they had started. They created that obligation, acted on it, had it reemphasized for them by the researcher, shifted responsibility to the researcher or to the learner for the learner's being shocked, questioned whether they should continue, wrestled with that powerfully felt obligation as they experienced the resistance of the learner, and at times abandoned that obligation and stopped. Ordinary people did all this (Miller 1986, Higgins 1994, 16–17).

While ordinary people are capable of committing great harm, ordinary people hold to a different common sense. Recall that Milgram asked psychiatrists, college students, and middle-class adults whether they would shock the learner and whether people in general would shock the learner. These "other" ordinary people—who did not participate as the teacher in Milgram's research but were asked to respond about their and others' possible participation—could not imagine that they or others would shock the learner. They thought only a small percentage, 1 or 2 percent at most, would shock to the highest level. These ordinary people saw a wide gulf between themselves and those who would shockingly harm others. They were dramatically wrong. Their common sense failed them.

Ordinary people have a great capacity to harm others. By typically thinking otherwise, by separating "us" normal people from "those" deviants, we protect ourselves from seriously confronting our capabilities. Our common sense that normal people would not do that—whatever serious deviance is the focus—comforts us. For example, we look abroad to the horrors inflicted by warring factions in a distant country on one another, to the slaughter of tens of thousands, even hundreds of thousands, of people. We ask ourselves what kinds of people must they be to do such horrors? We answer that they must be savages, just look at them.

UNREMARKABLE HARM

But in looking at them, we fail to look at ourselves, at the "savagery" we ordinary people and our ordinary ancestors have committed. For example, during the European colonization of the Americas (or might it be called invasion), between 60 and 80 million indigenous people in Central America, South America, and the Indies perished before the seventeenth century. As many as 95 percent, even 99 percent, of indigenous people were exterminated in various parts of Central and South America in less than 100 years. While much of this genocide resulted from the spread of European diseases, the Europeans also worked the enslaved Amerindians to death or mass murdered them. European explorers chained the native people together at the neck, marched them to mines to labor, and decapitated those who did not walk fast enough. Those who reached the silver mines typically toiled for three to four months before they died. The slave drivers figured that it was cheaper to work tens of thousands of native people to death and then replace them than to support a permanent enslaved workforce. The explorers also "sliced off women's breasts for sport and fed their babies to the packs of armored wolfhounds and mastiffs that accompanied the Spanish soldiers" (Stannard 1992, 430).

The destruction of the native people in North America was as complete as it was to the south. Between the 1500s and the late 1800s, 97 percent to 99 percent of the 7 million to 18 million native population was exterminated. Again, much of the destruction resulted from the spread of disease. But the native people were also systematically killed so that the colonizers could control the land. The colonizers burned Indian towns and the surrounding cornfields, poisoned communities, murdered the native people, and sold Indian women and children into slavery in the Indies. William Bradford, the governor of Plymouth Colony, wrote of the reaction of settlers to one mass immolation:

> It was a fearful sight to see [the Indians] frying in the fire and the streams of blood quenching the same, and horrible was the stink and scent thereof; but the victory seemed sweet sacrifice, and [the settlers] gave praise thereof to God, who had wrought so wonderfully for them. (Stannard 1992, 432)

The effort to eradicate the native population of North America continued with the founding of the United States. Almost all of America's early leaders supported that extermination. Andrew Jackson particularly seemed to relish the challenge. He called native people "savage dogs," boasted of keeping the scalps of some of the native people he killed, and supervised the mutilation of about 800 Creek Indian corpses. The noses were cut off to document the number killed. Long strips from the bodies were sliced, tanned, and made into bridle reins. Another time, Jackson ordered his troops to kill all the Indian children they could find, along with the men and women, so that the Indians could not reestablish their population (Stannard 1992).

CONCLUSION

Ordinary people, not just deranged, psychotic people, commit tremendous harm. They do so when they create compelling understandings and feelings. Some of those compelling understandings and feelings may be widely accepted, legitimate. The harm then is not deviant, but perhaps even honorable. At other times, the compelling understandings and feelings are viewed by authorities and citizens as unacceptable, wrong, criminal, even abnormal. Certainly some who commit great harm are appropriately understood to be deeply disturbed. Yet, ironically, the harm that those who are deeply disturbed commit is often much more limited than that done by regular people in the name of a just cause.

A Jeffrey Dahmer is no match for the killing machine of European explorers, colonists, or warring factions throughout the world today. He cannot compare to Stalinist Russia in which tens of millions of people perished; to ordinary citizens in Nazi Germany who were Hitler's willing executioners (Goldhagen 1996); to the Japanese military and government before and during World War II who brutalized, raped, tortured, and killed millions of people in China and Asia, as well as committed unspeakable horrors against captured U.S. and other Allied armed services personnel; to enslavers throughout history and the world; and on and on (Higgins 1994, 1–2). And bystanders—other countries and their leaders—often looked at the horror committed elsewhere without intervening (Sobran 1997).

Ordinary people also commit more "mundane" harm, assaulting one another without too much reflection or concern. Much domestic violence is not taken to be violence at all (Straus 1994)! Yet, compared to past eras, people are harming one another less (Higgins 1994, 144, 150–53; Straus 1994, chap. 2). For that we can be grateful.

Now, what would you do if you were the teacher asked to shock a learner who makes mistakes? Are you having second thoughts?

PROJECTS

1. Ask a sample of individuals these questions: Who would knowingly, physically, significantly harm others? Who would do so to the death of the people harmed? Ask the individuals to write and explain their responses. Examine the responses. Can you usefully group the responses into different kinds? For example, maybe some responses focus on traits of the individual, such as mental health problems. Perhaps others stress reasons, such as seeking revenge. Some responses may point to experiences earlier in the people's lives that turn them into kinds of people who seriously harm others. You decide whether it is useful to group responses into categories that you create. Are some responses more prevalent than others? What proportion of the responses indicate that disturbed, abnormal people are the ones who seriously harm others? Do these responses that focus on disturbed people give any indication that more than the disturbed quality of the people is important when harm is committed? Did anyone indicate that ordinary people seriously harm others? What insights do you now have?

2. Explain Milgram's research to a sample of people, as I did to you. Ask that sample of people what they would do in the situation. How far would they shock the learner? Ask them what percentage of people they believe would shock to the highest level. Request that they explain their responses. Compare people's responses to Milgram's results. How able are people to imagine their actions in seemingly novel situations? If they explain deviance by referring to people with deviant traits, then are they likely to imagine that they and other ordinary people could commit the deviance? Does an explanation that stresses deviant traits separate "those" deviants from "us" conventional people? Does it lessen the likelihood that people will examine how individuals create meaningful experiences such that they commit deviance?

15

DO YOU GET THE TIME
BECAUSE YOU DID THE CRIME?

Imagine that an acquaintance of yours was recently put on probation after being arrested and pleading guilty to shoplifting. You encounter a friend who also knows the acquaintance and tell the friend that the acquaintance is on probation. The friend asks why. What's your response to your friend? Please formulate your response, then continue reading.

Did you respond to your friend in the following or similar way: The acquaintance was given probation because the acquaintance shoplifted? If you did, that seems reasonable.

I imagine that you have read, heard, or uttered statements similar to the following: The offender got (here can be put what the punishment was—expulsion, a fine, imprisonment of a certain length, probation, after-school detention, etc.) because the offender did (and here can be put the offender's deviance). For example, the student received detention because the student did not do the homework. Or the club member was expelled because the member did not pay the dues. Or the defendant was imprisoned because the defendant robbed a taxicab driver.

These and similar statements are unremarkable. We casually utter them and hear them. But do we think much about what they mean? Let's do so. What do those statements above mean? More specifically, what do those statements claim is the cause of the punishments to the offenders? After writing your response, please continue.

The statements above claim that the offenders' deviance caused the punishments the offenders received. For example, the

147

student received detention *because* the student did not do the homework. The failure to do the homework was the *cause of* receiving the detention. That is obvious, right. But does it make sense? Does the offender's behavior cause the punishment given by others? I don't think so. Let me explain.

THE CRIME DOESN'T CAUSE THE TIME

First, the actions of one person cannot cause others to behave in any specific way. Unless people are literally physically forced to act by a person, that person cannot make people act. The person can demand, urge, threaten, promise, and much more, but that person cannot cause or make others act. Others can always do otherwise, even if they may experience some unpleasant consequences (Higgins 1994, chap. 4). Therefore, the actions of the offenders—failing to do homework, not paying dues, robbing the taxicab driver—cannot compel others to punish the offenders in any particular way or to act in any specific way toward the offenders. Others can always act toward the offenders in a variety of ways, the specific punishment given this time being just one way.

You might object to my argument. You might complain that the statements do not claim that the offenders' behaviors literally caused others to punish the offenders in particular ways. Instead, the statements claim that the offenders' behaviors were the reasons for the punishment. On account of the offenders' behaviors, others detained, expelled, or imprisoned the offenders. This seems to be a promising objection. But I don't think it will succeed.

In attempting to soften the determinativeness of cause, this objection attributes to the offenders and their behavior what rightly belongs to those offended. Notice where responsibility for the punishment is put. The punishment is *due* to the offensive behavior. The offenders and their behavior are responsible for the punishments, according to the objection.

But this objection misplaces responsibility for the punishment. How can offenders be responsible for what punishers do to them? Offenders certainly can be responsible for what they do, but not for what others do to them that the offenders did not wish to be done to them.

When we assert or accept that the individuals were punished *because* they committed some acts, we have obscured what we believe we have explained. The individuals' acts do not explain why or how the punishers handled the offenders as they did.

Consider the student who did not do the homework. Sometimes teachers detain students who do not do their homework. Sometimes teachers punish students who do not do their homework by requiring them to do more homework, withholding recess, or in other ways. Sometimes teachers do not punish the students at all. How, then, can the failure to do the homework be the *reason for* or the *explanation for* the detention when apparently at another time the failure to do the homework is the *reason for* a different punishment or even the *reason for* no punishment. This reason or explanation is surely operating in an odd way.

Let me present an extended example to make the point that asserting that the deviance is the cause of, the reason for, or the explanation for the punishment is not useful. The assertion presents what needs to be explained as if it were the explanation.

AMERICA'S "WAR" ON DRUGS

Consider drug use. America's policy toward drug use has been complex and varied. Let me present a few highlights of that policy. America has promoted drug use, tolerated drug use, become intolerant of drug use, and prohibited the use of various drugs throughout its history. For example, throughout the 1800s opium and cocaine were sold openly in America. Opium and its derivatives were ingredients in painkillers available at the time. They were available without prescriptions in hundreds of medicines. Cocaine became popular as a tonic for sinusitis and hay fever and as a cure for opium, morphine, and alcohol habits. It became a favorite ingredient of medicines, soda pop, and other beverages (Musto 1987, chap. 1; Meier 1994, chap. 2).

One of the first national drug laws prohibited the importation of opium for smoking in 1909. The federal prohibition followed the actions of California and other western states. In the latter 1800s local ordinances in California prohibited the smoking of opium. In 1881 California banned smoking opium. Seventeen other western states also prohibited smoking opium. Notice that consuming opium by means other than smoking or importing opium for purposes other than smoking remained legal. Why?

These prohibitions were aimed at Chinese immigrants. The laws were part of an effort to drive out the Chinese or in other ways control them. Chinese immigrants had been brought to the western United States in the latter 1800s to help build the railroads and work in the gold and silver mines. When the railroads were finished and the mines became no longer productive, a depression ensued. With jobs scarce, the Chinese immigrants became an economic threat to American workers. The local and state prohibitions were part of an effort to control or eliminate that threat.

A small number of Chinese immigrants brought with them the practice of smoking opium. The employers of the Chinese immigrants encouraged that practice. Working conditions were unbelievably hard. Immigrants were without their families. Medical care was rare. Opium smoking lessened the psychological and physical pain of the workers. Employers profited from selling opium to the laborers. Finally, by threatening to withhold the opium, the employers were able to make the workers more compliant, lessening their expressed discontent (Chambliss 1977).

The Chinese practice of smoking opium had been cultivated by British and, to a lesser extent, American traders to China in the 1800s and by Portugese and other European traders during the previous several centuries. The opium trade was profitable for the British colonial empire. The British government in India "raised one-half of its operating revenues from the export of opium to China" (Meier 1994, 24). The Chinese, eventually realizing that they were trading away silver, silk, tea, and other important commodities for opium, tried to resist the importation of opium. From 1839 to 1842, Great Britain fought and won the infamous Opium Wars with China in order to preserve its "right" to import opium to China. As part of the settlement of the conflict, Great Britain was given possession of Hong Kong, which in 1997 it returned to China.

The United States enacted the federal prohibition against opium primarily because of economic concerns, not moral concerns. Elimination of the opium trade would reduce the British domination of general trade with China, increasing opportunities for American trade. The prohibition would improve relations with China, perhaps encouraging China to do more business with American firms. China was willing to reduce the immigration of its citizens to America if America helped reduce the importation of opium to China. The need for cheap Chinese labor had declined by the latter 1800s. The continuing immigration of Chinese workers had become the basis for economic conflict in the West. The United States organized a convention to restrict trade in smoking opium. During the convention, to show its good faith and to save face because it had no national prohibition, the United States quickly prohibited the importation of smoking opium (Chambliss 1977; Musto 1987; Meier 1994; Reinarman 1994). American authorities criminalized opium as a means to control "troublesome" people (i.e., people who are already seen for one reason or another as a threat to the dominant segment of society) during troubling times. The criminalization of other drugs can be understood similarly (Reinarman 1994).

The present controversy concerning the disparity in sentences given to those convicted of selling or using powder cocaine compared to those convicted of selling or using crack cocaine speaks to the inadequacy of claiming that the deviant behavior is the reason for the punishment. Federal statutes and the statutes of approximately a dozen states treat more harshly the possession of crack cocaine than powder cocaine. For example, under federal guidelines, the sale of five grams of crack, "barely a teaspoon," mandates a minimum sentence of five years for a first-time offender (Isikoff 1995). A first-time offender would have to sell one hundred times that amount of powder cocaine, 500 grams, to be subject to the same federal sentence. Five grams of crack cocaine produce ten to fifty doses and cost between $225 and $750. Five hundred grams of powder cocaine produce 2,500 to 5,000 doses and cost between $32,500 and $50,000 (U.S. Sentencing Commission 1995a, iii, viii). Federal conviction of a first offense of *simple possession* of five grams or more of crack cocaine *mandates* a *minimum* sentence of five years in prison. Federal conviction of simple possession of powder cocaine and any other drug by a first-time offender provides a *maximum* sentence of one year in prison (U.S. Sentencing Commission 1995a, iii).

The average prison sentence for a federal conviction of trafficking in crack cocaine from October 1, 1992, to September 30, 1993 (fiscal year 1993), was ten and one-half years; the average prison sentence was eight years for trafficking in powder cocaine. Eighty-eight percent of crack cocaine trafficking offenders were black; 4 percent were white. Thirty-two percent of powder cocaine trafficking offenders were white; 27 percent were black. The average prison sentence for a federal conviction of simple possession of crack cocaine was 30.6 months for fiscal year 1993; the average sentence for simple possession of powder cocaine was 3.2 months. Eighty-five percent of convicted offenders of simple possession of crack cocaine were black; 10 percent were white. Fifty-eight percent of convicted offenders of simple possession of powder cocaine were white; 27 percent were black (U.S. Sentencing Commission 1995a, chap. 7).

The differences in sentencing for the sale or possession of crack cocaine compared to the sale or possession of powder cocaine and the relation between those differences and who is convicted for those offenses—blacks or whites—concern some citizens and officials. Even though no discriminatory intent may exist, black drug offenders are subjected to harsher sentencing than are white drug offenders (in part) due to the differences in the sentencing of crack cocaine and powder cocaine offenders (U.S. Sentencing Commission 1995a, xi).

Given these few developments in America's drug policy that I have presented, how useful is it to claim that people are imprisoned *because* they use narcotics? Such a simple statement overlooks America's changing policies toward drugs and the contexts and concerns out of which America changed its policies. Such a simple statement overlooks that for much of America's history people who used narcotics were not punished. Narcotics use was not even deviant.

Let's accept the present state of the historically changing drug policy in America as given (not as something to be explained) and focus on the handling of drug offenses. Even then, the claim that particular people are punished in whatever way they are punished *because* of their drug offenses does not explain the punishments. Such a simple statement overlooks the local context and concerns in which officials, law enforcement officers, judges, users, attorneys, and others produce punishments this time for these offenders. It overlooks the actions, reactions, and interactions of the participants as they produce the particular punishments. It overlooks what may be a system of justice designed to control and discipline the "urban underclass," those "who are perceived as dangerous" because of their marginal ties to conventional society and their involvement with the criminal justice system (McConville and Mirsky 1995, 217).

CONCLUSION

Casually, unthinkingly, we use and are told the "explanation" that people are punished because of their deviance: The person who thinks himself or herself to be a world leader is committed to a mental health facility because of the delusion. The child is sent to his or her room because of the sassy backtalk. The employee is fired because of the drinking problems. The driver is fined because of failing to stop at a stop sign. The student is expelled because of bringing a weapon to school. The convicted killer is executed because of the double murder. And on and on.

These statements do not help us understand how and why people who acted in various ways were punished. They are comforting, however. The statements tell us that the people punished "brought it on themselves." By putting the responsibility for the punishment on those punished, these statements deflect our attention from the concerns, interests, and maneuverings of the punishers.

But don't misunderstand me. I am not arguing that those who commit deviance are not responsible for their actions. I am not arguing that offenders should or should not be punished. I am trying to encourage us not to be satisfied with "explanations" that do not explain. I am trying to encourage us to think carefully and critically about how people who act in various ways come to be punished. Their actions do not explain the punishments.

To explain what is done to an offender, we may wish to examine how the behavior the offender did came to be made deviant in the place where it occurred. How did particular punishments, 154 for that behavior become established? Finally, how did this offender at this time come to be punished as he or she was punished?

When you next encounter the claim that someone was punished because of his or her deviance, try to investigate that punishment. Investigate who participated in producing that punishment. What were their concerns as they managed the incident? What reasoning did they use in their maneuverings? What policy existed to "cover" the situation? How was that policy used? What could the participants have done? Whose interests were served in producing the particular punishment? These and other questions can guide your thinking about the punishment of deviance.

Return to the question which this essay poses: do you get the time *because* you did the crime? What do you think now?

PROJECT

1. Examine the options that judges, members of disciplinary boards, or others who deal with deviance have for handling cases that come before them. Do they have only one option for handling cases of the "same kind"? Do they have a variety of options? If you can talk with judges, members of disciplinary boards, or others who deal with deviance, such as school principals, discuss how and why they dealt with particular cases of deviance as they did. This could certainly be difficult to discuss. Questioning people about their decisions may imply that you are criticizing their decisions. Also, people may not be able to recall well, may not have reflected carefully on, or be able to explain, how and why they dealt with deviance as they did. You might compare how judges, members of disciplinary boards, or others who have responsibility for dealing with deviance do so in one place compared to another. For example, you could compare how two school boards deal with infractions of school district policy or two principals do so. Have someone else help you with the investigation for this comparison. If apparently similar instances of deviance are handled differently in different places, then can you conclude that the punishment was *only* the result of the deviance? If not, then can you investigate what may have led to the differing ways that officials in different organizations deal with seemingly similar instances of deviance? What insights do you develop?

16

CAN WE DEAL WITH DEVIANCE
WITHOUT DISCRIMINATING?

Many people are concerned that how officials and others deal with deviance is discriminatory. Consider the following items:

The late Richard M. Nixon, former president of the United States, was pardoned for any offense he committed in connection with the scandal known as Watergate. Virglio Gonzalez, one of the men who broke into the Democratic National Committee's headquarters in the Watergate complex, served fifteen months in prison (Reiman 1995, 130–31).

Charles Bazarian, convicted of "swindling" $20 million from two California savings and loan institutions and other fraud, served less than two years in prison (Reiman 1995, 128). The typical convicted robber will serve an average of five years in prison (Reiman 1995, 125).

Sylvester Adams, a mentally retarded black man who had been severely abused growing up, was executed a couple of years ago in South Carolina for killing a sixteen-year-old neighbor. At the time of the murder, Adams was twenty-three. Less than a month before Adams's execution, Susan Smith, a 23-year-old white woman well known in her South Carolina community, was sentenced to two life terms in prison for drowning her two young sons by strapping them in their car seats and rolling the car into a lake. The case received national attention (O'Shea, LeBlanc, and Decker 1995d; Greene and Allard 1995).

156

Many people are concerned that the criminal justice system discriminates. The rioting that occurred after the not-guilty verdicts in the first trial concerning the four police officers in Los Angeles who "beat" Rodney King speaks to the rage and depth of that concern. Many believe that if you wear a business suit and steal millions of dollars, you may serve at most a few years in prison. More likely, you may plea-bargain to receive probation and to pay a seemingly large fine of tens of thousands, even hundreds of thousands, of dollars that you may not actually pay. But if you wear a mask and steal a few thousand dollars, you may be put behind bars for years or even for life (Reiman 1995).

Others look to the disparate federal sentences mandated for the possession or sale of crack cocaine compared to the sentences mandated for the possession or sale of powder cocaine as further evidence of discrimination in how deviance is handled. Recall my discussion of the disparate sentences in the previous chapter. The U.S. Sentencing Commission recently recommended to Congress that penalties for dealing crack cocaine be made more similar to penalties for powder cocaine (*The State* 1997e). Other observers disagree that officials discriminate when handling deviance (Wilbanks, 1987).

Whether one agrees or disagrees that discrimination is pervasive within the criminal justice system and within other arenas where we handle deviance, most observers assume that we should not discriminate. "Identical" deviance should be handled in "identical" ways. That's fair! Perhaps in past eras people intentionally discriminated, but we are trying to, or should be trying to, root out all discrimination. Discrimination has no place in dealing with deviance, according to this well-meaning sentiment (Black 1989, chap. 1).

Perhaps a different, nonobvious view is needed concerning discrimination and how we deal with deviance. This contrasting view reminds us that deviance is an integral feature of social life. Social life cannot exist without deviance. Further, this alternative view emphasizes the strong bond between the structure of social life and the structure of dealing with deviance. Each grows out of and gives rise to the other. I develop this view more fully after I present a hypothetical situation.

HOW WOULD YOU HANDLE THIS?

Consider the following hypothetical situation. Put yourself in the position of the person below who must decide what to do. Some people will have experienced such a situation or learned of such a situation. Others will have experienced very similar situations. Of course, what people think they might do and what they indeed do when involved in an actual situation may be very different. Nevertheless, here is the situation:

> You drive with a friend [consider one of your closest friends for this scenario] to a nearby store to buy a [you fill in the blank]. While looking for that item and at other merchandise, you notice that your friend has picked up a [you fill in this item], casually examined it, and stuck it in her or his pocket. The friend does not return the item to the counter. Instead, the friend starts to walk out of the store with it.

What do you do? Please write your response and explain it. Take it as seriously as you can. Then continue.

I imagine that you may have had some difficulty deciding what to do. Maybe you couldn't believe what you had seen. Thinking you were mistaken, you decided just to drop the whole thing. Perhaps you considered confronting your friend about the item shoplifted. Maybe you decided to talk with your friend, urging her or him to return the item. Perhaps you decided not to get involved. Did you consider telling store personnel about your friend's shoplifting? Probably not. I think it would be hard to decide what to do.

Now imagine a similar scenario: You have gone into a store to buy some merchandise. You see a stranger about your age pick up an item, examine it, then pocket it. Near to you is a store clerk or manager who did not witness the event. What do you do? Please consider this scenario as carefully as you can, then write your response and reasoning. When you are finished, continue reading.

Again, did you have some difficulty deciding what to do? Did you decide to stay out of it? If so, why? Or did you decide to intervene, perhaps telling the store employee what you had seen? Perhaps you stared at the stranger, hoping that your disapproval would shame the stranger into returning the item. I doubt that you decided to tell the person who shoplifted that you had seen her or him and that she or he should put back the item.

Compare how you thought you would handle the two shoplifting scenarios involving your friend and the stranger. Did you decide to handle the two scenarios differently? For example, did you decide to "go easy" on your friend but turn in the stranger who shoplifted? If so, how do you feel about not handling the two situations in the same way?

To see how a variety of people may respond to these two scenarios, you can conduct some research. Write up the two scenarios. Provide some alternatives for handling the situations from which the respondents can select one. Or allow the respondents to decide without any alternatives listed how they will handle the situations. Present one or the other scenario, not both, to a sample of people. For example, perhaps ask twenty people to respond to the shoplifting that involves the friend, another twenty to the shoplifting that involves the stranger. I imagine that you will find that people in general respond less harshly to the friend than to the stranger.

That is what I found when I asked students to respond to one of the scenarios. Just one of the seventeen students who responded to the scenario involving a friend said that he or she would tell store personnel about the friend's shoplifting—and this would be done only after talking to the friend and the friend's refusal to return the item. Many of the students who read the scenario in which they witnessed the stranger shoplifting also would not tell store personnel. As some wrote, it is not their business, or one never knows how the stranger may react. But *35 percent* of the students (six out of seventeen) said that they would tell store personnel. If you find what my results showed—and that is what Donald Black (1976, 1989) would expect—then what might you say about whether ordinary people, not just officials, discriminate when dealing with deviance?

JURISPRUDENTIAL VERSUS SOCIOLOGICAL VIEW
OF HANDLING DEVIANCE

Many people are concerned that how officials and others deal with deviance is discriminatory. Identical deviance appears not to be handled in identical ways. Who you are and who you know seem to matter, according to many critics of how deviance is handled. This concern applies to the criminal justice system, the mental health system, the juvenile justice system, disciplinary boards, as well as other realms in which deviance is handled. As I revise this chapter, some observers of the army are concerned that African-American drill sergeants are being targeted and discriminated against as the army investigates and prosecutes officers who have been accused of violating military regulations governing sexual conduct with enlisted soldiers, including sexual assault (Ruane 1997). While some observers disagree that how deviance is handled is discriminatory (cf Wilbanks, 1987), I believe that the evidence strongly indicates that discrimination occurs (Black 1976, 1989, 1993; Reiman 1995).

The title of this chapter poses a question: can we deal with deviance without discriminating? It is a more perplexing question than whether or not we discriminate. To me, the evidence indicates that discrimination occurs—and not so infrequently that we can dismiss the discrimination as insignificant. The question, can we deal with deviance without discriminating? points to a more fundamental basis for the existing discrimination. If it did not, then the "quick-and-easy" response would be that, of course, we can handle deviance without discriminating. All we need to do is discover where it occurs and put a stop to it. I do not think a "quick-and-easy" response is adequate. I imagine that you do not either. I believe that the more adequate response is that it is almost impossible for people to deal with deviance without discriminating. But why?

To explain why the "quick-and-easy" response is not satisfactory and that the "almost impossible" response may be more adequate if also troubling, I briefly present two contrasting views of the law, a jurisprudential model and a sociological model. My discussion uses the work of Donald Black (1976; 1989, chap. 1;

1993). While my discussion focuses on the law, these two views can be applied more generally to any means intended for rationally dealing with deviance. After explaining these two contrasting views, I indicate how we can apply them to other realms for dealing with deviance.

The *jurisprudential model* of the law emphasizes that law is a logical process. "The facts of each case are assessed in light of the applicable rules, and logic determines the results" (Black 1989, 20). The same facts of the offense should result in the same legal outcome. Law is meant to be universal. It is available to all and meant to be applied in the same way at all times. This jurisprudential model emphasizes how cases should be decided within rational, logical law.

Discrimination in handling deviance is an aberration as understood by this jurisprudential model. Discrimination is an unwelcome deviation from rational, logical law. It should be corrected. Only the facts of the case and the rational application of the law should matter in dealing with deviance.

In stark contrast to the jurisprudential model of the law stands the *sociological model*. The sociological model regards the law not merely as an abstract, rational body of rules. Instead, law is what people do when they "legally" handle (or do not handle) people's behavior (Black 1989, 20). A sociological view does not assume that law is rational, universal, impartial. It does not focus on how deviance should be handled. Instead, a sociological model seeks to explain how deviance is handled. It explores how people legally act. Do witnesses or victims call the police or not? Do the police respond when called? Do the police arrest a suspect or warn a suspect? Do prosecutors plea-bargain or take the case to trial? Do juries convict or acquit? What, if any, punishment does the judge dispense? A sociological model argues that how deviance is legally handled depends importantly on the *social structure of the case*.

The social structure of the case is the web of social relations among the parties involved in the case. Let's focus first on a complainant and the person against whom the complaint is lodged, such as the victim of an alleged theft and the alleged thief. What is the *social status* of the victim and the alleged offender? Social status describes one's standing in the community. Wealth, education, and respectability may be thought of as three dimensions of social status. Other dimensions could be explored. Social status varies. People may have more or less social status—more or less wealth, education, and respectability.

Some observers claim that those with low social status are discriminated against by the criminal justice system. For example, poor people or minority citizens are discriminated against, critics claim. Other observers argue that such discrimination does not occur or is not widespread. The critics and the defenders of the justice system are overlooking the social structure of the case.

The social structure of the case does not focus on the social characteristics of the parties as individuals. Instead, it focuses on the social characteristics of the parties in relation to one another. It focuses on the web of relations. Thus, do the complainant and the offender have (approximately) equal social status? If so, is it equally high or equally low? If their social statuses are different, then who has the higher social status, who the lower? The victim and the offender may be unskilled laborers. Or the victim may be an upper-middle-class professional, and the offender may be someone who has not held a regular job for years. How deviance will be handled depends on the relative social status of the parties involved.

The *relational distance* among the parties involved is another feature of the social structure of the case. How socially close are the parties involved? Are they family, friends, acquaintances, or strangers? Deviance is likely to be handled less formally, less harshly when intimates are involved than when strangers are involved. When family members assault one another, the police are less likely to arrest than when strangers assault one another (Black 1976, chap. 3).

Recall how you handled the theft by your friend and the theft by a stranger. The difference between the two incidents in the relational distance of the involved parties would suggest that you or others would be less likely to turn in a friend than a stranger. That is what I found when I asked students to respond to one of the two scenarios.

And social structure can be thought of in other ways, such as how *organized* the involved parties are. A company is more organized than an individual. The more organized a participant is in a dispute, the more likely that the participant will succeed in the dispute (Black 1976, chap. 5; 1989, chap. 3).

But the social structure of the case involves more than the complainant and who is complained against. Other parties may be involved and their relative social characteristics are important for determining the social structure of the case. Lawyers, supporters, witnesses, judges, and juries all bring their social status, relational distance, and other social characteristics to the case. The social structure of the case becomes more complex. For example, the victim and the accused may be strangers. Yet the victim may be well known by the jury in a small town, but the offender may be a stranger to the jury.

The sociological model of the law assumes that how a case of deviance is handled "always reflects the social characteristics of those involved in it" (Black 1989, 21). The social structures of cases that are "technically" identical can vary greatly. When social diversity exists, discrimination will occur in handling deviance!

Thus, the sociological model does not see discrimination as an aberration, as an unfortunate deviation from how the law should work. Instead, the sociological model sees discrimination as something to be expected when social diversity exists. A sociological model does not condone discrimination; however, it understands discrimination to be embedded in the social diversity of society.

CAPITAL PUNISHMENT AND THE SOCIAL STRUCTURE OF HOMICIDE

Let me present an investigation that illustrates that how deviance is dealt with depends on the social structure of the case. Consider capital punishment. Controversy surrounds its use. A significant part of that controversy is the differential use of capital punishment.

In Georgia, Florida, and Illinois from 1976 through 1980, *white* homicide suspects were *more* likely to be sentenced to death than *black* homicide suspects (Gross and Mauro 1989). Does that make sense? Perhaps the criticism that black people are more harshly treated by the justice system than are white people is simply wrong. Recall, however, that the relationship among the parties involved is crucial, not just the characteristics of specific individuals.

Black people who killed white individuals in Georgia, Florida, and Illinois were more likely to receive the death penalty than white people who killed white individuals in those three states. In Georgia, 20.1 percent of black defendants who killed white people received death sentences; 5.7 percent of white suspects who killed white people received the death penalty. In Florida, 13.7 percent of black defendants who killed white victims received a death sentence; 5.2 percent of white defendants who killed white victims received a death sentence. In Illinois, the comparable percentages were 7.5 percent and 1.9 percent (Gross and Mauro 1989, 45).

The differences in percentages may seem small, but we might focus on the ratio of the percentages, not their differences. In Georgia, black defendants who killed white people were *three and one-half times* as likely as white defendants who killed white people to be sentenced to death. In Florida, black defendants who killed white victims were *two and one-half times* as likely as white defendants who killed white people to be sentenced to death. Black defendants in Illinois who killed white people were almost *four times* as likely as white defendants who killed white people to be sentenced to death. Black defendants who killed white people were much more likely to be sentenced to death in those three states than were white defendants who killed white people.

Donald Black (1976, 1989) argues that, when someone of lower status commits deviance against a person of higher status, the deviant is more likely to be handled harshly than when someone commits deviance against a person of equal status. Using race as a measure of status in America, those who are white generally have higher status than those who are black. Consequently, Black would expect—and the research results support him—that death sentences would more likely be given when black defendants kill white victims than when white defendants kill white victims (with all else equal, such as the aggravating or mitigating circumstances of the crime).

More generally, Black argues that deviance by a low-status person against a high-status person will receive the most use of law; deviance by a high- status person against another high-status person will receive the next most use of law; deviance by a low-status person against another low-status person will receive less law; and, finally, deviance by a high-status person against a low-status person will receive the least law. The use of capital punishment in Georgia, Florida, and Illinois supports Black's argument well, though not completely (Gross and Mauro 1989).

Recall once again that Black argues that the structure of the case is important for how deviance is handled. That structure of the case is the web of relations among all the parties involved, including the lawyers, the judge, the jury, and still others, not just the victim and the offender. The research that has explored the use of capital punishment in Georgia, Florida, and Illinois examines only part of that web of relationships.

We may be appalled that death sentences are more likely to be given when a black person kills a white individual than when a white person kills a black individual. Yet, as Black (1989, 21) points out, every legal system handles cases differently according to the web of relationships among the parties involved. We should not expect cases that involve "identical" deviance but differ according to the structure of relations to be handled the same. Instead, we should expect discrimination. And that is what we observe everywhere!

For example, the Code of Hammurabi, compiled 4,000 years ago in Babylonia, provided a different response to violations based on the structure of relations among the parties involved. A man who struck someone his equal was required to pay one *mana* of silver. But a man who struck his superior would be publicly whipped sixty times with an ox-tail. Among the Nuer of Sudan, the killing of a stranger, especially a foreigner who does not come within the "most extended form of the social structure," is not wrong. The killing of a fellow tribesman, which is a private wrong, may require retaliation or restitution. The closer the relation among the killer's and the victim's tribal segments, the more likely restitution will be appropriate. Among close blood relationships, restitution becomes less necessary as the people who assist the offender to pay are the recipients of the restitution. Finally, if a man kills his wife, which is very rare, he would pay nothing because the restitution would be paid to himself (Black 1989, 98–99).

Not only does the law discriminate, but so, too, does every system for dealing with deviance (Black 1989, 102). Wherever people have created differences among one another—differences of social status, relational distance, and other social characteristics—the handling of deviance reflects the web of relations of the parties involved in the deviance. It reflects the relations among the deviants, victims, witnesses, supporters, advocates, and controllers of the deviance. We should expect that how school officials handle student deviance, how the juvenile justice system handles the delinquency of youths, how disciplinary boards handle the deviance of the members of the organization, how the mental health system handles the aberrant behavior of citizens, and how people handle deviance in whatever realm will reflect the web of relations among the parties involved.

SHOPLIFTING AND THE SOCIAL STRUCTURE OF THE CASE

Let's return to shoplifting and explore how the social structure of the case matters in dealing with deviance. More than twenty years ago, two social scientists observed how shoppers reacted to (staged) instances of shoplifting (Steffensmeier and Terry 1973). The social scientists were not interested in whether people responded differently to friends or strangers who shoplifted. All the shoplifters (actually assistants of the social scientists) were strangers to the customers. Instead, they were interested in whether shoplifters who appeared to be "hippies"—soiled patched jeans, well-worn shoes with no socks, long and unruly hair—were more likely to be reported than those who appeared to be "straight"—neatly pressed slacks, sport jacket and tie, short hair if a man, or dress, fur coat, and well groomed if a woman.

Whom do you think shoppers were more likely to report to store personnel: the hippie shoplifters or the straight shoplifters? If you think shoppers were more likely to report hippie shoplifters, you are right. Now, how can we make sense of this in terms of the social structure of the case? Please consider your response, then continue.

The shoppers were middle-class, conventional citizens. Based on appearance, the hippie shoplifters had less social status than did the shoppers; the straight shoplifters had similar social status as the shoppers. When responding to hippie shoplifters, the shoppers were responding to someone with less social status. When responding to the straight shoplifters, they were responding to someone with similar social status. The social structure of the case—as it concerned the offender and the witness—differed when the shoplifter appeared to be a hippie or straight. Complaints are more likely to be made against someone lower in social status than against someone similar or higher in social status (Black 1976, chap. 2).

THE STRUCTURE OF SOCIAL LIFE, THE STRUCTURE OF HANDLING DEVIANCE

As I noted at the beginning of this chapter and as I explored more fully in an earlier chapter, deviance is an integral feature of social life. Social life cannot exist without deviance. Through deviance—through making some human activity unacceptable—people structure how they will act and give meaning to themselves.

All members of a group arrange themselves in relation to one another. They organize themselves "above," "below," and equal to one another; "near" to and "far" from one another; and in other ways. All social life is structured through patterns of relations (Black 1993, Appendix). No people treat one another as if all are the same. For example, those in authority give orders;

subordinates follow orders. To give orders that others accept makes the order giver an authority and the order followers subordinates. Or one does favors for an intimate that one would not do for a stranger. To treat a stranger exactly as one treats an intimate would make both of them the same, neither stranger nor intimate. To almost all of us that would be absurd!

How people deal with deviance reflects and helps create the structure of social life. And by handling deviance differently depending on the web of relations among the parties involved, those people are supporting the existing structure of social life.

What can we do if we wish to reduce or eliminate that discrimination? Often people wring their hands and proclaim that all people must be treated equally. To be treated equally often means that equally harsh punishment must be given to all. The idea is to use more law to improve the shortcomings of law (Black 1989, chap. 5). But would we eliminate differential handling by using more law than we at present do? Probably not. As long as cases are socially diverse—possessing differing webs of relationships—the handling of those cases will be discriminatory.

How, then, can we reduce or eliminate discrimination in the handling of deviance? If differential handling reflects social diversity among cases of deviance, then social diversity may need to be eliminated. To the extent that cases are socially similar, then with all else equal, how they are handled will be similar, too. But how can we create cases that are socially similar?

Perhaps we could manipulate the social characteristics of the parties involved so that social diversity is reduced. For example, individuals who bring complaints against organizations or have organizations bring complaints against them are at a great disadvantage. Individuals have fewer resources to pursue their complaints or defend themselves, their credibility is questioned, they are less effective in supporting their interests. Perhaps legal coops could be established so that, in becoming members, individuals could enjoy the benefits of organizations in dealing with deviance. Individuals would become more socially similar to organizations. With social diversity lessened, discriminatory handling of deviance would decrease (Black 1989, chap. 3).

Perhaps knowledge of social characteristics could be lessened or eliminated. Even though social diversity among the parties would exist, if those deciding the cases knew little or nothing of that diversity, then differential dealing would decrease. That seems to happen already with parking tickets. While one may draw some conclusions about the social characteristics of the drivers from the parked cars, cars are much less informative about the social characteristics of their drivers than are the drivers themselves. Thus, parking justice may be much less discriminatory than other kinds of justice. But in a small town where police often know who drives what car, social diversity of parking violators is more apparent and differential handling more prevalent (Black 1989, 62–63).

If society can develop ways to reduce the amount of information that those who handle deviance have about the web of relationships among the parties involved, then discrimination in handling deviance would decrease, according to Donald Black. Some means already exist. For example, judges may bar some social information from testimony as immaterial to the case, and "shield" laws exclude some information, such as information about a sexual assault victim's sexual history (Black 1989, 68). Can you think of other means for reducing the social diversity of cases of deviance?

CONCLUSION

Can we deal with deviance without discriminating? Yes, but only with great effort. Discrimination in handling deviance occurs as people create differences among one another. Discrimination reflects and supports the diversity of social life. People deal with deviance within a web of relations that may vary from one instance of deviance to another, seemingly identical instance. To reduce discrimination, we must reduce the basis for that discrimination.

We could try to reduce what those who handle deviance know about the web of relations among the parties involved. Or we can try to change the structure of social life so that differences in the webs of relations among people decrease. What an awesome challenge! But we have done so.

Compared to past eras (consider the era of slavery as a stark example, but consider your lifetime, too), Americans do not interact with people of different ethnicities as unequally as they once did. Americans interact nowadays with people of different ethnicities more closely to how they interact with people similar in ethnicity than in the past. For example, half a century ago most white Americans thought that black people "should only get jobs whites didn't want. Now, almost no one feels that way" (Samuelson 1995, 215). Black and white Americans are more likely now to have a "close personal friend" of the "other race" than in the past (Samuelson 1995, 215). Finally, "only a fifth of white married couples ha[ve] husbands and wives of the same ethnic background" (Samuelson 1995, 215). Today, people of different ethnicities intermarry much more than in past eras. Americans also interact today with people of different social statuses more closely to how they interact with people of similar social statuses than they once did. In important ways Americans are structuring social life less unequally, less differentially than in past eras. Consequently, discrimination in dealing with deviance may have lessened (see Tittle, Villemez, and Smith 1978; but they do not focus clearly on the structure of the case).

Yes, we can deal with deviance without discriminating. As we structure social life less differentially, we will discriminate less when dealing with deviance.

PROJECTS

1. Try to investigate to what extent social communities or groups in modern society have explicitly stated the use of different punishments for offenses that involve different social structures. For example, examine the criminal law of your state to see whether different punishments are mandated for killing a fellow civilian compared to killing a law enforcement officer or other officials of the state. Does threatening a governor call for a different sanction than threatening a fellow civilian? You might examine the stated (or perhaps customary) penalties in a school district when a student hits another student or when a student hits a teacher or school official, or when a student steals from another student or steals from a teacher or school official. A disciplinary or honor code for colleges may also state different punishments for offenses with different social structures.

2. Create hypothetical scenarios of offenses in which you develop two different versions of the same offense. Make the two versions differ according to the social structure of the case. For example, a twenty-year-old man "assaults" his eighteen-year-old brother (don't use the word "assault," but describe a fight where the older brother beats up the younger brother), or in a bar a twenty-year-old man "assaults" an eighteen-year-old man who is a stranger. Have people read one or the other version of the pair. Provide possible responses as to what should be done or ask them to give you their responses. Tally the responses for the two separate versions. Compare your tallies. Does the social structure of the case make a difference?

17

EACH CASE OF DEVIANCE IS
DIFFERENT, ISN'T IT?

Judges, officers, disciplinary board members, principals, teachers, supervisors, officials of all kinds, and many other people have the difficult responsibility of handling those who have committed deviance. Judges and others who have that responsibility may do so regularly, as a routine part of their responsibilities. Do you think that those who regularly handle deviance should handle each case on its own merits? Each case should be considered carefully, then dealt with in the most appropriate manner. Let's explore this issue. Is each case, can each case, be handled "on its own merit"?

Imagine the following situation. You are a family court judge. Before you is a thirteen-year-old male youth. You have adjudicated him delinquent for breaking into a school and vandalizing several classrooms with two older youths, ages fifteen and sixteen. The damage is estimated at several thousand dollars. The youth had been detained for shoplifting when he was eleven, but he was let off with a warning when store officials decided not to prosecute, according to a police officer. The youth had also been put on community supervision last year for six months after being adjudicated delinquent for participating in taking a car to joyride. The car was driven around town until an officer spotted it weaving across lanes, pulled the driver over, and found several youths in it. The juvenile officer who evaluated the youth tells you that he lives with his aunt who cares deeply for him, but that she works two jobs and is not home much.

How will you handle the youth? Will you put the youth on community supervision, perhaps with stricter requirements for reporting to his supervisor and for his conduct? Or might you send him to the state's juvenile justice facility where he will likely spend about five to eight months? The state has just opened some alternative facilities so the youth could go to a wilderness camp instead of to a traditional institution. Would you like more information about the youth—about his family life, his school conduct, his attitude about life, his plans for the future, his behavior in his community, and so on before you decide? Would you like to talk with him in depth in order to get to know him before you make up your mind? Please think about how you would handle the youth, then continue.

Imagine that you decide to send him to one of the new wilderness camps run by the juvenile justice department. Months later, you learn that many of the youths sent to that wilderness camp seem to be doing well. Few disruptions occur at the camp, the first "graduates" of the camp have returned to their hometowns and local schools and have done satisfactorily. You are pleased with alternatives that the state has now provided for dealing with delinquent youths.

Let's continue this hypothetical situation. The following year, a fourteen-year-old youth comes before you. You adjudicate him delinquent for shoplifting some expensive sneakers. Eight months earlier, he had been put on community supervision for shoplifting some clothes. According to a police officer, he has been stopped for underage drinking a couple of times and released to the custody of his mother, a single parent with four children. She cleans office buildings downtown from 10 P.M. until 6 A.M. Her oldest child, eighteen, is expected to look after her siblings, but the eighteen-year-old is busy with school and a part-time job. How will you handle the youth? Will it be community supervision again or confinement to one of the facilities of the juvenile justice department, perhaps one of the wilderness camps or other alternative facilities? Please think about what you will do, then continue.

Let's keep the imagination going one step further. Imagine that many youths come before you each week, perhaps dozens do. Many present situations that remind you of the two youths above. Others appear quite different. How will you handle each of these youths, each of these cases? Will you handle each of them as unique cases, making your decision based on the particulars of each situation? That would seem fair to do. After all, each child is unique; each case is different.

Many of us may imagine that judges, officers, disciplinary board members, principals, and others who routinely handle deviance should treat each case as the unique situation it is assumed to be. When I ask my students whether they believe that each case should be handle as unique, they typically tell me yes. Yet, is it possible to do so? Would it be wise to try to do so? What do judges and others who regularly handle deviance do?

EACH CASE IS DIFFERENT—OR IS IT?

Is it possible to treat each case of deviance and each offender as a unique situation? No. Fundamentally, we don't live in a world of uniqueness; we live in a world of generalizations, of categories in which we organize our experience. When we speak of and act toward "tree," "car," "rock," "child who is running," "horrible," and all the other ways in which we categorize our experiences, we are no longer treating each experience as unique. We give the experiences meaning through the categorizes we use to shape the experiences, organize them, understand them. The categories ignore all the particulars of the experiences. The categories gloss over whatever differences we could identify among the instances placed in the categories and tie those instances together through a common meaning. Categories downplay uniqueness.

The child who is running is moving her or his body in some particular way. We organize our experience of it by calling it running. In doing so, we do not emphasize the uniqueness of the child's movement. Instead, we stress its fundamental similarity to other children and adults when they "run." When we state that children are running, we are treating all of the children's movements as if they were the same. We are not attending to whatever differences we could otherwise notice. The same is so for deviance.

Consider the hypothetical examples I asked you to imagine above. I spoke of such actions and objects as shoplifting, joyriding, vandalism, a thirteen-year-old youth (not adult), and so on. By using those categories in my hypothetical examples, I presented particular actions and people, not in their uniqueness, but in their similarities to other actions and people similarly categorized. This categorization is also done officially, as in the charging of a youth with shoplifting. Acts officially labeled shoplifting vary in unlimited ways. Officially labeling diverse acts as shoplifting deemphasizes uniqueness in favor of similarity and generality. The family court is organized to treat people of certain ages, typically sixteen or under, as similar in one important respect—they are not adults. So, fundamentally, it is not possible to treat each instance as unique. We do not organize our experiences that way. We do not live that way.

We certainly create differences between our experiences, in this instance between different cases of deviance. But we do so along dimensions by which we organize our experiences. We may create differences along such dimensions as what we see as the *seriousness of the offense*, the *character of the youth* (e.g., whether the youth is remorseful), the *support the youth has at home*, and still other dimensions. Those dimensions become the ways we understand the cases and the offenders, and they become features on which we partly decide how to handle the offenders and their offenses. Again, the many particulars that we could take into account are not taken into account.

To try to treat each case as unique (even though fundamentally that is not possible) would not make sense. To try to do so would mean that each time judges, officers, members of disciplinary boards, principals, or whoever must handle deviance had a case to handle, the decision makers could not use their experiences. They could not use how they handled previous cases and the outcomes of how they handled those previous cases in deciding how to handle this instance. They could not because each case is unique, or at least treated as so. Therefore, experience with prior cases would be of no use for handling present cases. If all cases are unique, then present cases have nothing in common with prior cases. Nothing can be learned from how previous cases were handled. The judges, officers, members of disciplinary boards, principals, and other handlers would be starting from "scratch," uninformed, inexperienced each time they handled cases *if* they tried to treat each case as unique. Do you find that absurd?

Instead, we expect those who handle deviance to handle similarly cases seen to be similar. We also expect those who handle deviance to learn from their experiences in order to handle future cases more successfully. Both these expectations indicate that we do not act as if cases are unique. Cases may differ, but they are not unique.

When we expect those who handle deviance to handle similar cases similarly, we are asking that fairness be upheld. A problem, however, is how to decide what cases are similar. Cases may be understood as similar in terms of the official categories of deviance in which they are placed, the amount of monetary loss, the degree of harm to people (e.g., how many people are hurt and to what extent), the prior record of the offender, the age of the offender, the social circumstance of the offender, the culpability of the offender, and on and on. Observers may see great similarities where others know that the differences are important. Therefore, how cases are handled may be seen as just or unjust depending on how observers see the cases as similar or different. The controversy over the greater sentences given to those convicted of possessing crack cocaine as compared to powdered cocaine, which I have written about in other chapters, speaks to the conflict over what is similar or different.

We expect those who handle deviance to learn from their prior experiences when they handle present cases. The only way to learn from their prior experiences is to be able to decide how present cases are similar to or different from prior cases. Doing that necessarily lessens whatever we mean by uniqueness in favor of categories, generalizations, comparability.

Return to the hypothetical scenario that started this chapter. When you learned that the wilderness camp was working well for many of the youth sent to it, did you use that information in deciding how to handle the second youth whose offense and situation could be seen as similar to that of the first youth? If so, then you were using prior experience in making your present decision, something that we expect when we are expected to be rational. To ignore prior experience would be foolish, perhaps even the basis for wondering about one's competence. It might even lead to one being treated as deviant.

Even if we believed that each case handled by judges, officers, members of disciplinary boards, principals, and others who deal with deviance should be handled uniquely, those who handle cases do not do so. Instead, they develop and use guidelines, rules of thumb, typical procedures for handling cases. In some fields these are officially mandated, as in federal and state sentencing guidelines. These and other guidelines, whether formal or informal, are used flexibly, not unthinkingly, mechanically.

For example, the U.S. Sentencing Commission, pursuant to federal law, has created and continues to revise a manual that federal courts must follow in sentencing federal offenders. As part of the manual, the commission has created a sentencing table that provides the range within which courts must sentence *each class* of convicted offenders unless atypical features are present. The sentencing table presents a grid of minimum to maximum sentences depending on the *offense level* of the charges for which the defendant was convicted and the *criminal history category* of the defendant. The offense levels run from 1 to 43. Criminal history categories run from category I to VI. For example, the guideline sentencing range for a defendant with an offense level of 17 and a criminal history category of II is 27 to 33 months imprisonment.

The sentencing commission determined base offense levels for federal offenses, which then could be adjusted up or down depending on particular features of the offense. For example, the base offense level for aggravated assault is 15. If the assault involved more than minimal planning, then the offense level will be increased by 2. The criminal history category classifies the defendant according to the defendant's prior record. The commission states that prior record increases the culpability of the defendant for the present offense. Repeated criminal behavior also indicates the lessened likelihood of successful rehabilitation. For example, for each prior sentence of imprisonment of more than one year and one month that the defendant has received, 3 points are to be added. Thus, a defendant with one prior sentence of imprisonment for three years who was convicted in federal court of aggravated assault in which more than minimal planning was involved (with no other features of the offense or of the defendant's prior record relevant to sentencing) would have an offense level of 17 and a criminal history category of II (2 or 3 points). As mentioned in the above paragraph, the appropriate sentence range in this case would be 27–33 months imprisonment (U.S. Sentencing Commission 1995b).

THEORY OF THE OFFICE

Officials use what has been called a "theory of the office" (Rubington and Weinberg 1978). They develop, learn from one another, and use a set of understandings, informal procedures, and unofficial routines in order to get their work done and in order to make sense of what they do. The theory of the office enables officials to give order to what otherwise could be chaotic. Some of the theory of the office may concern how to handle identified cases of deviance.

For example, several decades ago, judges in one municipal jurisdiction handled in a few hours the cases of as many as 250 people convicted for public drunkenness (Wiseman 1970, 85-100). Cases were disposed of in as little as thirty seconds. How was that possible? It was possible through a theory of the office in which judges treated each offender as one of about seven different types of drunks, with routine dispositions for each type. Judges classified those who were publicly drunk primarily on three characteristics: (1) general physical appearance (dirty, bloody, trembling, shaking, or not), (2) past performance (nature of past record of arrests for being drunk), and (3) social position (job, marital status, permanent address or not, down-and-out appearance). Judges created about seven different types of drunks based on combining these three features. Each type was likely to receive a particular disposition. For example, judges typically suspended the sentence for transients or put them on probation if they would leave town. They also typically suspended the sentence for "middle-aged repeaters" who had not come before them for a while but required the repeaters to attend alcoholism school or gave them to the custody of Christian missionaries. The "derelict-drunk" who is not gravely ill but is dirty, perhaps suffering withdrawal, and who may be malnourished was likely to be sentenced to jail in order to dry out. And so on.

Or consider how police in one southwestern city handled domestic violence several years ago (Ferraro 1989). The department adopted a presumptive arrest policy for domestic violence. Officers were directed to arrest domestic violence violators even when the victim did not desire prosecution. When probable cause existed, officers were expected to arrest the offender even if a misdemeanor offense was not committed in the officer's presence. But officers used their discretion in deciding how to handle domestic violence cases. For example, officers divided citizens into those who are "normal" and those who are deviant. Normal citizens work, have a family, don't typically become drunk, and keep their home at least modestly clean. They are understood by the police in this city to be white heterosexuals who speak English. Deviant citizens are unconventional, unacceptable. They are publicly drunk or high, homeless, involved in crime, live in dilapidated houses, have unusual family situations, and may not speak English well. Problems are a continuing part of their lives.

Police believe that arrest has substantially different consequences for normal citizens and deviant citizens. Normal citizens are typically law-abiding. They are shamed when arrested. Their deviance reflects situational stresses. Therefore, if the police arrest normal citizens who have committed domestic violence, the normal citizens may be less likely to commit domestic violence in the future. But violence and deviance are a way of life for deviant citizens, according to officers. Arrest is not unusual to them. It causes no shame. Therefore, arresting those who are termed "scum," "low lifes," or "those kind of people" is a waste of time. It will not do any good. Consequently, officers may less likely arrest deviant citizens who commit domestic violence than those who are seen to be normal citizens.

Research evaluating the consequences of arresting domestic violence offenders or handling the matter in other ways supports these officers' theory of the office, however distasteful its characterization of different segments of a community may be.

Men who have a greater stake in the conventional, mainstream community—through work and marriage—are less likely to commit domestic violence after being arrested compared to not being arrested. But those who are unemployed or are not married increase their domestic violence after being arrested (Sherman and Smith 1992; Berk et al. 1992). Perhaps these less "conventional" citizens are not shamed by arrest but are angered by it, as the theory of the office used by police officers in the southwestern city indicates.

CONCLUSION

Now, how would you handle cases of deviance? You may think that you should handle each case as unique. As I have explored, however, that is neither possible nor desirable. And that is not how officials of all kinds handle deviance. Instead, they use their and others' experience to handle cases routinely when possible. As they do so, they may classify cases into different kinds and handle cases they similarly classify in similar ways. Or they may use various understandings and procedures for dealing with cases. But they do not typically treat each instance of deviance as if it is unique. To understand how officials handle deviance, we need to explore the theories of the office that they use—and much more.

PROJECT

1. Talk with police officers, prosecuting attorneys, principals, disciplinary hearing officers, or other officials who routinely deal with deviance. Ask them to discuss how they handle various instances of deviance. Do they handle differently instances of what appear to be similar offenses that vary by other conditions? Do they use any "rules of thumb" in deciding how to deal with offenders? These rules of thumb may concern features of the cases and other issues in addition to characteristics of the offenses committed. Officials may categorize offenders as similar (or as different) based on features of the offenders, the offenders' social situation, and other matters and deal with "similar" offenders in similar ways.

18

IF WE SPARE THE ROD, WILL WE SPOIL THE CHILD?

How can people get others to act conventionally, to act in ways that the people find acceptable (Higgins 1994, chap. 4)? How can parents raise their children, teachers work with their students, bosses manage their workers? Many people believe that a firm hand, either literally or figuratively, is needed (Straus 1994). Some parents worry that law enforcement has tied their hands in disciplining their children. Educators may believe that with all the rights accorded students, the educators no longer have the means for effectively controlling their students. Bosses may wish that they could more easily fire unsatisfactory employees.

I do not take up all those issues in this chapter. Instead, I focus on physical punishment and on children. Will we spoil children if we spare the rod? While I focus on children, I think that the discussion pertains to other relations in which people try to control one another (Higgins 1994, chap. 4). I close this chapter with a brief discussion of how we might best raise children—and work with students, employees, and others.

HITTING CHILDREN, A NATIONAL PASTIME?

Raising children is challenging. It is to me and my wife. Most people experience that challenge. Raising children is challenging for many reasons. One is that children are not born naturally conventional, law-abiding. They have the capacity to become conventional members of their community. They also have the

182

capacity to act deviantly. Carefully observe young children. You will notice that they push, hit, grab, and use physical force to get what they want. They also assert themselves against limits. They defy the limits placed on them by parents and others through refusals, screams, ignoring, running away, and in other ways. The challenge is to raise children to become competent, caring, confident people.

You have heard the maxim Spare the rod and spoil the child. The maxim states that firm discipline is needed for children to develop satisfactorily. Firm discipline will instill in children respect for authority. It will teach children the consequences of unacceptable behavior. Children firmly punished will not desire to be punished again. Therefore, they will act appropriately. Without firm discipline, children will become unruly. They will become overly concerned with gratifying themselves. In past eras, parents did use rods to punish children. Today, all states allow parents to hit their children with physical objects, such as a belt or a paddle, "provided no serious injury results" (Straus 1994, 5). Rods, however, may no longer be appropriate.

What do you think about using physical punishment on children, perhaps using milder forms than a rod? Do you agree or disagree with the following three questions?

1. It is sometimes necessary to discipline a child with a good, hard spanking?
2. Spanking children helps them to be better people when they grow up.
3. Parents have a right to slap their teenage children who talk back to them.

Surveys asking these questions and others show that American adults strongly support the use of physical punishment against children. A 1986 national survey of adults showed that 84 percent agreed or strongly agreed that it is sometimes necessary to discipline a child with a good, hard spanking. That percentage is now about 65 percent (Schulte, 1997). A survey of New Hampshire parents indicated that 83 percent did *not* disagree with the statement that spanking children helps them to be better people when they grow up. And less than half the parents (47 percent) strongly disagreed with the statement that parents have a right to slap their teenage children who talk back to them (Straus 1991, 140).

American law permits physical punishment of children. The common law of every state does so. In the late 1960s child abuse legislation in all fifty states cracked down on what became seen as unacceptable treatment of children. But, that legislation made clear that parents retained the right to use physical punishment to discipline their children. For example, the New Hampshire Criminal Code states that parents, guardians, and others "responsible for the general care and welfare of a minor" are "justified in using force against such a minor when and to the extent that" they "reasonably" believe it is "necessary to prevent or punish such a minor's misconduct" (Straus 1991, 135). Teachers, too, in many states have the right to use physical punishment on students, though the number of states that allow teachers to use corporal punishment has declined from forty-six in 1979 to twenty-five in 1993 (Straus 1994, 172).

Not long ago in my community, a mother, summoned to her son's high school, slapped her son. A sheriff's deputy, stationed in the school, heard the slaps and arrested the mother. Controversy arose over what should be done. Other law enforcement officers intervened in the case. Eventually, the matter was dropped.

The most common physical punishments are "spanking, slapping, grabbing, and shoving a child 'roughly'—with more force than is needed to move the child" (Straus 1991, 134). Most parents use physical punishment against their children. Most people report having it used against them. For example, more than 90 percent of parents use physical punishment against children ages three and four. When children reach thirteen, about half of their parents use physical punishment against them. By age fifteen, one out of three children have parents who use physical punishment on them. And 95 percent of surveyed students in a community college indicated that they had experienced physical punishment (Straus 1991, 136).

Physical punishment, the "rod" if you will, is widely used and accepted in America and throughout the world. But not everywhere. Sweden in 1979 and the rest of Scandanavia and Austria in following years outlawed the spanking of children (Straus 1994, 170). Sweden's law is not designed to turn parents into criminals. It is not part of the criminal code. Instead, the law is designed to express the country's standards and to identify and assist parents who need help in managing their children (Straus, 1991: 136).

Does sparing the rod spoil the child? Or does using the rod damage the child? Recall that the maxim states that if strict discipline is not used, children will become unruly, self-centered, spoiled. They will not act as they should. But is that so? Or might physical punishment produce the consequences its supporters are trying to avoid?

THE UNINTENDED CONSEQUENCES OF PUNISHMENT

Physical punishment of children, especially when it is aggressively used as a dominant way of controlling children, "spoils" children. It damages them. It produces children who are more likely to act unacceptably, not less. For example, adults who were hit as adolescents are more likely to hit their spouses (Straus 1994, 104). The more that adults were physically punished as children, the greater the likelihood of assaulting people outside the family (Straus, 1991). Sons physically punished by their fathers are more likely to have a criminal record when they reach middle age than sons not physically punished by their fathers (McCord 1991).

Nevertheless, supporters of physical punishment and those skeptical of the research showing that physical punishment leads to worse behavior argue that the above evidence is not convincing. Adults who were physically punished in childhood and who are now acting less acceptably may have already been misbehaving as children more than those adults who were not physically punished in childhood. The physical punishment did not cause the youths to become adults who acted more unacceptably. They were already on a trajectory in childhood that resulted in their deviance as adults. Thus, the evidence is weak.

Studies that followed children with "severe behavior problems," however, found that when parents used corporal punishment or verbal aggression to control the "child's misbehavior, the child tried to use similar coercive tactics with the parents. The parents, of course, regarded this as more misbehavior and punished even more, and in turn the children became more coercive and hostile" (Straus 1994, 118). Getting parents to stop all corporal punishment can help break this vicious cycle (Straus 1994, 118–19).

A recent study shows that children aged six to nine, whose mothers did not use corporal punishment on them misbehaved less two years later than children of the same age whose mothers had used corporal punishment on them (Straus, Sugarman, and Giles-Sims 1997). This was so even after the degree of the children's misbehavior at the beginning of the two-year period was controlled in the comparison. This research may provide the strongest evidence to date that corporal punishment increases children's misbehavior.

But the controversy continues about the consequences of corporal punishment (Socolar et al. 1997). For example, some scholars thoughtfully argue that the context within which parents spank is significant for the consequences of the spanking on the children's subsequent behavior. To the extent that children see parents as legitimate authority figures and spanking as acceptable within their culture, then the children are likely to see being spanked as a "legitimate expression of parental authority." Spanking may improve their conduct. But to the extent that children do not see their parents as legitimate authority figures or do not see spanking as acceptable within their culture, then they are likely to see being spanked as parental aggression. Their subsequent behavior may become worse. For example, black children may see spanking as acceptable within their culture to a greater extent than do white children. If they do, then spanking may be more likely to improve the behavior of black children than the behavior of white children, especially when the spanking of black children is done by warm and reasoning parents (Gunnoe and Mariner 1997). The introduction of possible racial and ethnic differences in spanking makes the controversy over corporal punishment even more sensitive (Straus 1994, 184–86).

Most children who are physically punished do not become violent predators (Straus 1991, 1994). They live ordinary lives, filled with successes and setbacks. Hence, supporters of physical punishment often claim that they were physically punished as children and turned out all right. Therefore, physical punishment works. It is even necessary. But is it? Was it because of or despite the physical punishment that those physically punished as children turned out all right (Straus 1994, 116-17)? And children hit even a few times by their parents are slightly more likely to abuse their own children physically, to experience depressive symptoms, and commit "violence and crime later in life" (Straus 1994, 155).

Using the rod (i.e., physically punishing), not sparing the rod, may spoil the child. Why? Consider force. How do you respond when others order you to act in a particular way and threaten you if you do not? They may threaten to punish you physically or to restrict you in some way. How do you react if you are physically punished or restricted? Record your thoughts, then continue. Do you become more willing to do what others order you to do, or do you become resentful, mad, even hateful? Do you do your best at what you are ordered to do, or do you do just enough in order not to suffer the threats? Do you try to flee? If you cannot or do not leave, do you "escape" inside of yourself, shutting out the person who threatens you? Do you resist, perhaps fighting back against the person forcing you to act? To the extent that force is a key component of the relation between you and the other person wielding the force, then force is not likely to work well. It does not produce cooperation. It destroys it (Collins 1992, 65–69).

Physical punishment, one main form of force, is used to manipulate people, not to work together with them. Severe physical punishment may lead children to comply momentarily. But when the children are less likely to be detected, they will more likely behave as they have been ordered not to act. Punishment encourages children to do what will avoid pain for themselves. Therefore, it teaches children to be self-interested, to be concerned about their welfare, not the welfare of others. Using punishment also teaches children that giving pain is a legitimate way to get others to do what you want them to do (McCord, 1991).

If physical punishment has unintended, unwanted consequences, then perhaps parents and others should use nonphysical punishment in order to discipline children. Parents could send their children to their rooms, not allow them to watch television, not permit them to use the family car, and impose many other restrictions without physically assaulting them. What do you think?

Nonphysical punishment sounds promising. Through it, parents can discipline their children without physically hurting or intimidating them. Parents would not be teaching their children to hit, punch, kick or physically assault others in order to get others to do what one wants. Nonphysical punishment, especially when it is used heavy-handedly, still tells children that it is legitimate to impose pain on others in order to get others to do what one wants. Nonphysical punishment, especially when it is the dominant means of raising children, still teaches children to be concerned about their welfare. Nonphysical punishment may be an improvement over physical punishment, but as a primary means of raising children it suffers from some of the same shortcomings as does physical punishment (McCord 1991).

If not punishment, then why not rewards? Why not promise to reward children for doing what they are told to do, not threaten to punish them for failing to do what they are told to do? Provide children with money, privileges, and other payoffs for doing what is expected? Doesn't that sound better than punishments? What do you think? Those who hold dearly to the maxim Spare the rod and spoil the child are not likely to embrace rewards. They may respond that rewards will spoil the children. Children should not be rewarded for what is required of them. They should just do it, the supporters of punishment may claim.

I do not know whether rewards will spoil children, though research shows that paying off children to perform lessens their interest in what they are doing (Kohn 1993). But rewards are quite similar to punishment in what they do to children and what they tell children. Rewards manipulate, as does punishment. Rewards tell children that they will receive something desired only if they do what others tell them to do. Punishment embraces the same logic. If you do what you are told, then you will not receive some unpleasant consequences. Rewards, like punishment, tell children that it is legitimate to manipulate people. Rewards teach children to enhance *their* pleasure; punishment teaches them to lessen *their* pain. Neither encourages children to be concerned about the welfare of others (McCord 1991; Kohn 1993).

CONCLUSION

If we spare the rod, will we spoil the child? Not necessarily. Children can be raised successfully by parents who do not use physical punishment. *But if we primarily use the rod to raise children, we will more likely damage the children.* And important research strongly indicates that moderate or even minimal corporal punishment may have detrimental consequences for the development of children. Even rewards, if they are the primary means for controlling children, do not work well. They are similar to punishments. What, then, are parents to do?

When parents *accept* their children—affectionately interacting with them and responding to their emotional needs—are *firm* without being harsh with their children—clearly expecting them to act in a moral, responsible way—and encourage *autonomy*— supporting their children's growing self-direction, then children are most likely to become competent, caring, confident people (Steinberg 1996, chaps. 6 and 7). Such "authoritative" or "responsive" parenting is more effective than "authoritarian" or "permissive" parenting. Parents who use authoritarian means to control their children try to dominate their children, demanding that their children submit to the parents' often arbitrary and/or rigid rules. Parents who are permissive in their control allow their children to have their way. They may avoid "setting limits and engaging in conflicts" with their children in order to keep their children from being unhappy (Steinberg 1996, 112).

For example, permissive parents may overlook their teenagers' coming home after their curfew. These parents may not wish to upset their children. Authoritarian parents may quickly, harshly punish their children for their curfew violation, even one of a few minutes. These parents are showing their children who is in charge. Authoritative or responsive parents may talk with their children about the reasons for being late, the adequacy of the reasons, and the importance for calling to inform the parents before coming home late. The parents will discipline their children to the extent that they believe the violation warrants it, perhaps asking for their children's serious suggestions for possible consequences. These parents emphasize responsibility and regard for others (Steinberg 1996, 113–14).

Punishments and payoffs do not work as well as people imagine in raising successful children. Instead, acceptance, clear expectations, and support for autonomy work much better. But this may also be so for enabling students, employees, members of organizations, and others to behave appropriately, to perform their best (Kohn 1993; Steinberg 1996). What do you think?

PROJECTS

1. To learn to what extent people support the use of physical punishment on children, survey a sample of people. This could be a sample of people in one of your classes. Ask them to strongly agree, agree, disagree, or strongly disagree with the three statements mentioned in the chapter:

(A) It is sometimes necessary to discipline a child with a good, hard spanking.
(B) Spanking children helps them to be better people when they grow up.
(C) Parents have a right to slap their teenage children who talk back to them.

To explore this issue farther, you could compare groups of people who differ according to social experiences that you believe would be important in their developing beliefs about spanking or using other forms of corporal punishment on children. For example, perhaps those who had been physically punished as children may develop different beliefs from those who had not been physically punished as children (Straus, 1994: 57). Young adults may have different beliefs from those who are middle aged or who are or have been parents (Straus, 1994: 55–56).

2. Develop various scenarios in which children are misbehaving, perhaps from what you consider trivial misbehavior to more serious misbehavior. (Realize that how you evaluate the seriousness of the misbehavior may not be how others would.) Or the misbehavior could be done in the home or in public. You decide how the scenarios vary. Ask people to indicate how as parents they would handle the misbehaviors described in the scenarios. In which scenarios are the respondents more likely to say that they would use physical punishment? How do they account for their responses? What thoughts do you now have about controlling, punishing children?

3. A companion activity to project 2 would be to develop scenarios of misbehavior in which the parent's or adult's response to the child was stated. Similar misbehaviors could be presented with different parental responses. Spanking or other corporal punishments, as well as noncorporal discipline, could be included. Ask different samples of people to read the different scenarios to evaluate the appropriateness of the parental response to the misbehavior. Do they agree or disagree with how the hypothetical parents responded to the misbehaving child? What ideas do you develop about people's beliefs on punishing children?

4. Observe carefully in stores and other public places. How do parents handle the misbehavior of their children? If they use physical punishment, how do bystanders react? If any intervene, how do the punishing parents respond to the bystanders (Davis, 1991)? What insights do you develop about controlling children in public?

CONCLUSION

Deviance fascinates us and troubles us. We hold many assumptions about it. We may not consider carefully what we think about it. I have invited you to think about deviance in nonobvious ways, in ways that challenge what we take to be so. To do so may have been difficult, even troubling. To do so may ultimately be more useful. In particular, through your reading you have thought about the following:

Chapter 1: We may assume that some acts and attributes are inherently deviant, that the very nature of the acts and attributes makes that so. But it may be more useful to consider that through their negative reactions, people make acts and attributes deviant. How, then, do people come to react negatively to some behavior and not other behavior?

Chapter 2: Our first impression may be that people on the fringe of society are the ones who are deviant. Yet we all act, think, or possess characteristics to which others have reacted or do react negatively. We, ordinary people, are the deviants. We may be surprised to know that a significant percentage of ordinary people are even involved in deviance that is widely seen as serious—crime, alcohol problems, mental health difficulties, and illegal drug use, to name four. Thus, to think about deviance is to think about us, not just "them."

Chapter 3: Many of us wonder about why people commit deviance. In order to understand deviance more fully, however, we may wish to examine how people produce and participate in the phenomenon of deviance. We may wish to explore the processes through which people create deviance. What consequences do we create through those processes and for whom?

Chapter 4: Our first reaction may be that deviance is an unhealthy aberration in social life or at least an unwanted feature of social life. Yet we may also understand deviance to be a powerful means for creating social life, for enabling people to live and act together, for giving meaning to their lives. Social life cannot exist without deviance. How, then, do people use deviance to mold social life?

Chapter 5: Some behaviors, such as cannibalism and infanticide, disgust us. Yet these behaviors that are obviously horrendous to us are part of the natural capacity of humans. Moreover, some societies have accepted, even expected, their members to commit such behaviors. But other societies have transformed these behaviors that are part of humans' natural capacity into an abomination. What awesome ability people have to shape what is human! How do people make disgusting what is part of humans' natural capacity? How do other people make it required?

Chapter 6: While we may agree that much deviance harms people and social life, we may not realize that deviance may also be helpful. It can contribute to the production of social life. How so? Do people unequally benefit from this contribution?

Chapter 7: Further, instead of seeing deviance primarily as a violation of morality, we can also understand much of it as an attempt to uphold conventional morality. Even serious deviance may at times be usefully viewed as a means of social control, controlling the unacceptable behaviors of others. How do observers and officials react to this moralistic deviance? Through what other lenses can we view deviance?

Chapter 8: Knowing the amount of deviance that occurs is important for officials, policymakers, scholars, and citizens. They use that amount and related information in various ways. Many of us realize that trying to learn the true amount is difficult, if not impossible. It may be impossible because no actual amount exists independent of people who are interested in that issue. Officials, scholars, and other interested people produce the amount of deviance that they claim exists. How is the amount produced, how could it be produced, what difference does it matter how it is produced, and what are the consequences of producing the amount one way or another?

Chapter 9: What causes people to commit deviance? Social scientists have developed various explanations. But the concept of cause may not be particularly useful. Instead, how do people move themselves into deviance? What compelling feelings and thoughts enable people at this moment and place to commit deviance? How do those feelings and thoughts manage challenges that arise out of the larger social circumstances within which people live?

Chapter 10: Offenders must act, they must do something, in order to commit many kinds of deviance. The deviance does not just happen. Nevertheless, a crucial part of committing deviance is producing meanings—understandings and feelings—that enable participants to commit deviance at this place and time. Deviance is committed not only through movement but also through meaning. But how?

Chapter 11: We are likely to assume that either an instance of deviance occurred or did not occur, even though only the participants may know what really happened. A nonobvious approach may be more useful. An event does not announce to observers—or to its participants—what it is. Instead, observers, and even participants, always face the troubling responsibility of giving meaning to the events, of deciding what happened. Only after the event has occurred, sometimes years later, does what deviance it is come to exist. How do observers—and participants—decide what happened? How do they manage conflicts concerning this issue?

Chapter 12: Officials, counselors, family members, and many others who interact with offenders often wonder who the offender is. What kind of person is the offender? The offender "is" who the officials, counselors and other interested parties make the offender to be. Interested parties give offenders their identities. Defenders and detractors of the offenders may participate in identity contests, striving to have their proffered identities accepted as the true identities. How are the identities of deviants constructed?

Chapter 13: Without realizing it, we have and use images of harm. For example, when we think of crimes, we are likely to think of robbery, burglary, assault, and other street offenses. When we think of criminals, we are likely to think of young, low-income, often minority-group men living in the city. These typical images are the product of the workings of our society and of our justice system. But these images deflect our attention from equal, if not more serious, harm done elsewhere by business-people, professionals, government officials, and others who are successful. How do people use these typical images in furthering their interests in deviance, and how are we diversely affected by these typical images?

Chapter 14: Most of us cannot imagine seriously, intentionally harming others. Only disturbed people could do so. As Stanley Milgram's famous research indicates, however, ordinary people have a great capacity to harm others. The history of harm that people of one ethnic, religious, tribal, or other group have done to those of another group also points to the great capacity of ordinary people to inflict tremendous harm on others. Yes, harm is committed by people who are widely recognized as psychologically disturbed. But most harm is not. Most harm is committed by ordinary people who encounter and create social situations in which committing harm is understandable, doable, even laudable or necessary.

Chapter 15: You have likely heard, read, and/or used the statement that the offender received the time (i.e., punishment) because the offender did the crime (i.e., the deviance). But does such a statement explain why and how the reaction came to be, or does it obscure what it is meant to explain? A person's behavior does not dictate how others will react to it. For example, seemingly similar drug use has been over time and is at present handled in various ways. How do citizens and officials come to handle particular behavior as they do?

Chapter 16: Many people believe that we should not discriminate when dealing with deviance. Those who commit similar deviance should be handled in similar ways. As long as people differentiate themselves, creating differences among themselves, such as differences in status or in relational distance, people will also create differences in how they handle seemingly similar deviance. People deal with deviance within a structure of relationships among the participants. If the structure of the relationships differs from one instance of deviance to another seemingly similar instance of deviance, reactions will likely differ, too. Discrimination in dealing with deviance expresses the differentiated relationships that people have created. Such discrimination also helps to reproduce that differentiation. What can be done to reduce discrimination when dealing with deviance?

Chapter 17: In our society, which stresses individualism, with a heavy emphasis on the uniqueness of each individual and on the responsibility of people as individuals to make their own way, we may believe that each instance of deviance is unique, that each should be handled on its own individual merits. Yet is that possible? Is it desirable? Deviance, like life, exists through generalities, through categorizations, not uniqueness. How do those who manage deviance come to understand and handle specific events as instances of one kind of deviance but not another?

Chapter 18: Do we spoil the child if we spare the rod? More generally, is physical punishment an effective means for getting people to act conventionally or, to put it more directly, to do as those in charge wish? To the extent that physical punishment becomes the primary means of control, children and others are more likely, not less likely, to become spoiled humans. They become damaged people. Instead, acceptance, clear expectations that are upheld, and support for the individual's autonomy work best.

PRODUCING DEVIANCE, AN UNRECOGNIZED RESPONSIBILITY

All the chapters point to nonobvious ways of thinking about deviance. Woven throughout them is a common thread. This thread may at first have been overlooked. Once pointed out to us, we may be able to see it easily. But we may see it simply, not recognizing its complexity, not recognizing its profound implications for us.

The common thread in thinking about deviance and the most nonobvious way to do so is to examine continually, doggedly *how people produce deviance.* Deviance and all that it involves, all of its processes, do not somehow just happen. Neither nature nor the divine dictates what people produce. Neither conditions of the environment nor characteristics of people produce deviance. Instead, people do. We are completely responsible in every way imaginable for deviance.

People create deviance as they try to live and act with one another when nothing compels how they do live and act together. They create deviance as they give their lives meaning when nothing forces them to give any particular meaning to their and others' existence. The next moment in the drama of life, in the drama of deviance, is always made, not predetermined.

People produce deviance without the benefit of ever being able to compare what they have done to some absolute standard of what should have been done. Whatever certainty they create in producing deviance, they must do so and maintain for themselves. And they grapple, too, with their inability to create that certainty.

But each individual does not do all this alone, on her or his own. Instead, individuals produce deviance within social worlds—worlds of families, organizations, societies, and more. These worlds have been made, are maintained, are challenged, and even are changed by the individuals and by others. Individuals enter those worlds—at birth, when going to school, when making a new group of friends, when joining an organization, and in other ways. Individuals become who they are within these worlds. And as they do so, they and the others produce the dramas of deviance.

People produce deviance, each moment, often without much awareness of the awesomeness of their handiwork. They are caught up within the social life of their worlds. They do not step back to observe and think about what they and others do to produce deviance within those worlds, which they also fashion. Perhaps this book will help you to step back and think about deviance.

We think about deviance in order to think about ourselves, about our particular self and about our fellow producers of this awesome drama of life. By doing so, we may be able to produce more satisfying lives for ourselves and others. What do you think?

PROJECT

1. As you think about deviance, what questions do you now have about deviance, especially ones that you did not have before? What assumptions or beliefs about deviance that you had before reading this work do you now question? Why? Have you discarded any? Please explain. What are you now thinking about deviance?

REFERENCES

Adler, Patricia A. 1985. *Wheeling and Dealing: An Ethnography of an Upper-Level Drug Dealing and Smuggling Community.* New York: Columbia University Press.

Allard, John. 1994. "State to Keep Samples of Sex Offenders' DNA," *The State,* October 31, A1, A5.

Allison, Julie A., and Lawrence S. Wrightsman. 1993. *Rape: The Misunderstood Crime.* Newbury Park, Calif.: Sage.

Annin, Peter, and Kendall Hamilton. 1996. "Marriage or Rape?" *Newsweek,* December 16, 78.

Arbetter, Lisa. 1994. "Attitude and Theft: Partners in Crime." *Security Management* 38 (April): 12.

Athens, Lonnie H. 1989. *The Creation of Dangerous Violent Criminals.* London: Routledge.

Baker, Phyllis L. 1997. "And I Went Back: Battered Women's Negotiation of Choice." *Journal of Contemporary Ethnography* 26 (April): 55–74.

Banisky, Sandy. 1995. "N.J. Town's Ban on Foul Language Has Cleared Air." *The State,* February 6, A1, A6.

Beckett, Katherine. 1994. "Setting the Public Agenda: 'Street Crime' and Drug Use in American Politics." *Social Problems* 41 (August): 425–47.

Berk, Richard A., Alec Campbell, Ruth Klap, and Bruce Western. 1992. "The Deterrent Effect of Arrest in Incidents of Domestic Violence: A Bayesian Analysis of Four Field Experiments." *American Sociological Review* 57 (October): 698–708.

Berman, Pat. 1994. "Residents Air Concern on Man among Them with Violent History." *The State,* November 1, B4.

Best, Joel, and David F. Luckenbill. 1994. *Organizing Deviance.* 2nd ed. Englewood Cliffs, N.J.: Prentice Hall.

Black, Donald. 1976. *The Behavior of Law.* New York: Academic Press.

—— 1983. "Crime as Social Control." *American Sociological Review* 48 (February), 34–45.

—— 1989. *Sociological Justice.* New York: Oxford University Press.

—— 1993. *The Social Structure of Right and Wrong.* San Diego: Academic Press.

Chambliss, William J. 1977. "Markets, Profits, Labor and Smack." *Contemporary Crises* 1: 53–76.

Chubbuck, Katharine. 1997. "Houses of Horror." *Newsweek*, February 10, 40, 42.

Cohen, Albert K. 1966. *Deviance and Control*. Englewood Cliffs, N.J.: Prentice Hall.

Collins, Randall. 1992. *Sociological Insight: An Introduction to Non-Obvious Sociology*. 2nd ed. New York: Oxford University Press.

Coser, Lewis A. 1962. "Some Functions of Deviant Behavior and Normative Flexibility." *American Journal of Sociology* 68 (September): 172–81.

Cullen, Francis T. 1984. *Rethinking Crime and Deviance Theory: The Emergence of a Structuring Tradition*. Totowa, N.J.: Rowman & Allanheld.

Davis, Kingsley. 1937. "The Sociology of Prostitution." *American Sociological Review* 2 (October): 744–55.

Davis, Phillip W. 1991. "Stranger Intervention into Child Punishment in Public Places." *Social Problems* 38 (May): 227–46.

Decker, Twila. 1994. "Gail Cutro Convicted of Murder." *The State*, December 20, A1, A13.

—— 1995. "Facts Will Let Lawyers Mold 2 Faces for Smith." *The State*, April 16, A1, A10.

Dentler, Robert A., and Kai T. Erikson. 1959. "The Functions of Deviance in Groups." *Social Problems* 7 (Fall): 98–107.

Douglas, Jack D. 1977. "Shame and Deceit in Creative Deviance." Pp. 59–86 in *Deviance and Social Change*, ed. by Edward Sagarin. Beverly Hills, Calif.: Sage.

Durkheim, Emile. 1966. *The Rules of Sociological Method*. 8th ed. Trans. by Sarah A. Solovay and John H. Mueller; ed.by George E.G. Catlin. New York: Free Press.

Ek, Carl A., and Lala Carr Steelman. 1988. "Becoming a Runaway: From the Accounts of Youthful Runners." *Youth & Society* 16 (March): 334–58.

Elliott, Delbert S., and Suzanne S. Ageton. 1980. "Reconciling Race and Class Differences in Self-Reported and Official Estimates of Delinquency." *American Sociological Review* 45 (February): 95–110.

Emerson, Robert M. 1969. *Judging Delinquents: Context and Process in Juvenile Court*. Chicago: Aldine.

Empey, LaMar T. 1978. *American Delinquency: Its Meaning and Construction*. Homewood, Ill.: Dorsey Press.

Erikson, Kai T. 1962. "Notes on the Sociology of Deviance." *Social Problems* 9 (Spring):307–14.

Federal Bureau of Investigation. 1994. *Uniform Crime Reports for the United States 1993*. Washington, D.C.: U.S. Department of Justice.

—— 1995. *Uniform Crime Reports for the United States 1994*. Washington, D.C.: U. S. Department of Justice.

Felson, Marcus. 1994. *Crime and Everyday Life: Insight and Implications for Society*. Thousand Oaks, Calif.: Pine Forge.

Ferraro, Kathleen J. 1989. "Policing Woman Battering." *Social Problems* 36 (February): 61–74.

Ferraro, Kathleen J., and John M. Johnson. 1983. "How Women Experience Battering: The Process of Victimization." *Social Problems* 30 (February): 325–339.

Flanagan, Timothy J., and Kathleen Maguire, eds. 1990. *Sourcebook of Criminal Justice Statistics*. U.S. Department of Justice, Bureau of Justice Statistics. Washington, D.C.: Government Printing Office.

Frohmann, Lisa. 1991. "Discrediting Victims' Allegations of Sexual Assault: Prosecutorial Accounts of Case Rejections." *Social Problems* 38 (May): 213–26.

Gabor, Thomas. 1994. *'Everybody Does It!' Crime by the Public*. Toronto: University of Toronto Press.

Gallup, George Jr. 1996. *The Gallup Poll: Public Opinion 1995*. Wilmington, D.E.: Scholarly Resources Inc.

Garcia, Kimberly. 1992. "Grand Jury Decides Not to Indict on Rape Charge." *Austin American-Statesman*, October 9, A1, A8.

Goldhagen, Daniel Jonah. 1996. *Hitler's Willing Executioners: Ordinary Germans and the Holocaust*. New York: Knopf.

Goleman, Daniel. 1994. "Survey: Satanic Ritual Abuse Seldom Found." *The State*, October 31, A1, A5.

Goode, Erich. 1978. *Deviant Behavior: An Interactionist Approach*. Englewood Cliffs, N.J.: Prentice Hall.

—— 1994. *Deviant Behavior*. 4th ed. Englewood Cliffs, N.J.: Prentice Hall.

Goodman, Ellen. 1996. "We Must Go After the Men Who Go After the Young Girls." *The State*, February 9, A12.

Gordon-Grube, Karen. 1988. "Anthropology in Post-Renaissance Europe: The Tradition of Medicinal Cannibalism." *American Anthropologist* 90 (June): 405–9.

Gottfredson, Michael R., and Travis Hirschi. 1990. *A General Theory of Crime*. Stanford, Calif: Stanford University Press.

Gould, Stephen Jay. 1978. "Biological Potential vs. Biological Deter-
minism." Pp. 343–51 in *The Sociobiology Debate*, ed. by A.L. Ca-
plan. New York: Harper & Row.

―― 1981. *The Mismeasure of Man*. New York: Norton.

Greene, Lisa. 1995. "Teen Not Guilty in Killing." *The State*, October 28,
A1, A8.

Greene, Lisa, and John Allard. 1995. "Troubled Mind, Violent Life
Scarred Adams, Lawyer Says." *The State*, August 13, A1, A14.

Gross, Samuel R., and Robert Mauro. 1989. *Death and Discrimination:
Racial Disparities in Capital Sentencing*. Boston: Northeastern
University Press.

Gunnoe, Marjorie Lindner, and Carrie Lea Mariner. 1997. "Toward a De-
velopmental-Contextual Model of the Effects of Parental Spanking
on Children's Aggression." *Archives of Pediatrics & Adolescent
Medicine* 151 (August): 768–75.

Harris, Marvin. 1989. *Our Kind: Who We Are, Where We Came From,
and Where We Are Going*. New York: HarperCollins.

Herdt, Gilbert H. 1984. *Ritualized Homosexuality in Melanesia*.
Berkeley: University of California Press.

Hewitt, Kim. 1997. *Mutilating the Body: Identity in Blood and Ink*.
Bowling Green, Ohio: Bowling Green State University Popular
Press.

Higgins, Paul. 1994. *Sociological Wonderment: The Puzzles of Social
Life*. Los Angeles: Roxbury.

Higgins, Paul C., and Richard R. Butler. 1982. *Understanding Deviance*.
New York: McGraw-Hill.

Hindelang, Michael J., Travis Hirschi, and Joseph G. Weis. 1981. *Mea-
suring Delinquency*. Beverly Hills, Calif.: Sage.

Hogsett, Randall M. III, and William J. Radig. 1994. "Employee Crime:
The Cost and Some Control Measures." *Review of Business* 16
(Winter): 9–14.

Hollinger, Richard C., and John P. Clark. 1983. *Theft by Employees*. Lexington, Mass.: D.C. Heath.

Inciardi, James A. 1992. *The War on Drugs II: The Continuing Epic of
Heroin, Cocaine, Crack, Crime, AIDS, and Public Policy*. Moun-
tain View, Calif.: Mayfield.

Isikoff, Michael. 1995. "Crack, Coke and Race." *Newsweek*, November
6, 77.

Jankowski, Martín Sánchez. 1991. *Islands in the Street: Gangs and
American Urban Society*. Berkeley: University of California Press.

Johnston, Lloyd D., Patrick M. O'Malley, and Jerald G. Bachman. 1996. *National Survey Results on Drug Use from the Monitoring The Future Study, 1975–1994*. Rockville, Md.: National Institute on Drug Abuse, National Institutes of Health, No. 96–4027.

Jones, Del. 1997. "48% of Workers Admit to Unethical or Illegal Acts." *USA Today*, April 4, 1A, 2A.

Katz, Jack. 1988. *Seductions of Crime: Moral and Sensual Attractions in Doing Evil*. New York: Basic Books.

Keil, Richard. 1993. "Few Paying S & L Fines That Kept Them out of Jail." *The State*, February 25, 1A, 10A.

Kitsuse, John I., and Aaron V. Cicourel. 1963. "A Note on the Uses of Official Statistics." *Social Problems* 11 (Fall): 131–9.

Klemmack, Susan H., and David L. Klemmack. 1976. "The Social Definition of Rape." Pp. 135–147 in *Sexual Assault: The Victim and the Rapist*, eds. Marcia J. Walker and Stanley L. Brodsky. Lexington, Mass.: D.C. Heath.

Klockars, Carl B. 1974. *The Professional Fence*. New York: Free Press.

Kohn, Alfie. 1993. *Punished by Rewards: The Trouble with Gold Stars, Incentive Plans, A's, Praise, and Other Bribes*. Boston: Houghton Mifflin.

LeBlanc, Clif. 1994a. "Sheriff to Pump Up Pressure Against Loud Music, Speeders." *The State*, October 20, B2.

—— 1994b. "Expert Says Babies Died of SIDS." *The State*, December 9, A1, A9.

—— 1995. "Plant Has Record of Violations." *The State*, September 19, B1, B5.

Lejeune, Robert. 1977. "The Management of a Mugging." *Urban Life* 6 (July): 123–48.

Lejeune, Robert, and Nicolas Alex. 1973. "On Being Mugged: The Event and Its Aftermath." *Urban Life and Culture* 2 (October): 259–87.

Lenski, Gerhard, Jean Lenski, and Patrick Nolan. 1991. *Human Societies: An Introduction to Macrosociology* 6th ed. New York: McGraw-Hill.

Letkemann, Peter. 1973. *Crime as Work*. Englewood Cliffs, NJ: Prentice Hall.

Liazos, Alexander. 1972. "The Poverty of the Sociology of Deviance: Nuts, Sluts, and Preverts." *Social Problems* 20 (Summer): 103–20.

Link, Bruce G., Francis T. Cullen, Elmer Struening, Patrick E. Shrout, and Bruce P. Dohrenwend. 1989. "A Modified Labeling Theory

Approach to Mental Disorders: An Empirical Assessment." *American Sociological Review* 54 (June): 400–423.

Liska, Allen E., and William Baccaglini. 1990. "Feeling Safe by Comparison: Crime in the Newspapers." *Social Problems* 37 (August): 360–74.

Loseke, Donileen R. 1992. *The Battered Woman and Shelters: The Social Construction of Wife Abuse*. Albany, N.Y.: State University of New York Press.

Luckenbill, David F. 1977. "Criminal Homicide as a Situated Transaction." *Social Problems* 25 (December): 176–86.

McCaffrey, Barry R. 1997. "We're on a Perilous Path." *Newsweek*, February 3, 27.

McCleary, Richard, Barbara C. Nienstedt, and James M. Erven. 1982. "Uniform Crime Reports as Organizational Outcomes: Three Time Series Experiments." *Social Problems* 29 (April): 361–72.

McConville, Mike, and Chester Mirsky. 1995. "Guilty Plea Courts: A Social Disciplinary Model of Criminal Justice." *Social Problems* 42 (May): 216–34.

McCord, Joan. 1991. "Questioning the Value of Punishment." *Social Problems* 38 (May): 167–79.

Mead, George H. 1918. "The Psychology of Punitive Justice." *American Journal of Sociology* 23 (March): 577–602.

Meier, Kenneth J. 1994. *The Politics of Sin: Drugs, Alcohol, and Public Policy*. Armonk, N.Y.: M.E. Sharpe.

Merriam-Webster. 1986. *Webster's Third New International Dictionary*. Springfield, Mass.: Merriam-Webster.

Merton, Robert K. 1957. *Social Theory and Social Structure*. Rev. ed. Glencoe, Ill.: Free Press.

Meyer, Michael. 1994. "Crimes of the 'Net.'" *Newsweek*, November 14, 46–47.

Michael, Robert T., John H. Gagnon, Edward O. Laumann, and Gina Kolata. 1994. *Sex in America: A Definitive Survey*. Boston: Little, Brown.

Milgram, Stanley. 1974. *Obedience to Authority: An Experimental View*. New York: Harper & Row.

Miller, Dan. 1986. "Milgram Redux: Obedience and Disobedience in Authority Relations." Pp. 77–105 in *Studies in Symbolic Interaction*, vol. 7, ed. Norman K. Denzin. Greenwich, Conn.: JAI Press.

Milloy, Ross E. 1992. "Furor Over a Decision Not to Indict in a Rape Case." *New York Times*, October 25, Sec. 1, 30L.

Morganthau, Tom. 1997. "The War Over Weed." *Newsweek*. February 3, 20–22.

Morris, Aldon D. 1984. *The Origins of the Civil Rights Movement: Black Communities Organizing for Change*. New York: Free Press.

Musto, David F. 1987. *The American Disease: Origins Of Narcotic Control*. Expanded ed. New York: Oxford University Press.

New York Times. 1992. "2nd Jury Charges Man in Condom-Rape Case." October 28, A15.

O'Shea, Margaret N., Clif LeBlanc, and Twila Decker. 1995a. "Jurors Join Dad's Tears for Lost Boys." *The State*, July 26, A1, A6.

—— 1995b. "Jurors Glimpse Smith's Sons in Life and Death." *The State*, July 27, A1, A8.

—— 1995c. "'I Failed': Stepfather Faces Jury." *The State*, July 28, A1, A7.

—— 1995d. "Mother Gets Two Life Terms; Boys' Father Tries to Forgive." *The State*, July 29, A1, A10.

Patterson, Lezlie. 1998. "Is School Crime On the Rise?" *The State*, January 22, B1, B7.

Perkins, Craig A., Patsy A. Klaus, Lisa D. Bastian, and Robyn L. Cohen. 1996. "Criminal Victimization in the United States, 1993." Bureau of Justice Statistics, U.S. Department of Justice, Washington, D.C.

Pfuhl, Erdwin H., and Stuart Henry. 1993. *The Deviance Process*. 3rd ed. New York: Aldine de Gruyter.

Phillips, Jim. 1993. "Man Convicted in Condom Rape: Sentencing Today." *Austin American-Statesman*, May 14, A1, A19.

Phillips, Jim, and Kimberly Garcia. 1992. "Grand Jury Indicts Man in Condom Rape Case." *Austin American-Statesman*, October 28, A1, A6.

Plate, Thomas. 1975. *Crime Pays! An Inside Look at Burglars, Car Thieves, Loan Sharks, Hit Men, Fences, and Other Professionals in Crime*. New York: Simon and Schuster.

Reiman, Jeffrey. 1995. *The Rich Get Richer and the Poor Get Prison: Ideology, Class, and Criminal Justice*. 4th ed. Boston: Allyn & Bacon.

Reinarman, Craig. 1994. "The Social Construction of Drug Scares." Pp. 92–104 in *Constructions of Deviance: Social Power, Context, and Interaction*, eds. Patricia A. Adler and Peter Adler. Belmont, Calif.: Wadsworth.

Richards, Pamela, Richard A. Berk, and Brenda Forster. 1979. *Crime as Play: Delinquency in a Middle Class Suburb*. Cambridge, Mass.: Ballinger.

Rouse, Beatrice A., ed. 1995. *Substance Abuse and Mental Health Sta-tistics Sourcebook*. DHHS Publication No. (SMA) 95–3064 Wash-ington, D.C.: Government Printing Office.

Ruane, Michael E. 1997. "Soldier Sentenced for Rapes, Abuse." *The State*, May 7, A1, A9.

Rubington, Earl, and Martin S. Weinberg. 1978. *Deviance: The Interac-tionist Perspective*. 3rd ed. New York: Macmillan.

Sampson, Robert J., and John H . Laub. 1993. *Crime in the Making: Pathways and Turning Points Through Life*. Cambridge: Harvard University Press.

Samuelson, Robert J. 1995. *The Good Life and Its Discontents: The American Dream in the Age of Entitlement, 1945–1995*. New York: Time Books.

Schulte, Brigid. 1997. "Sparing the Rod Actually Helps the Child, Study Says." *The State*, August 15, A1, A13.

Sherman, Lawrence W., and Douglas A. Smith, with Janell D. Schmidt and Dennis P. Rogan. 1992. "Crime, Punishment, and Stake in Conformity: Legal and Informal Control of Domestic Violence." *American Sociological Review* 57 (October): 680–90.

Simmons, J.L. 1965. "Public Stereotypes of Deviants." *Social Problems* 13 (Fall): 223–32.

Smith, Douglas A., and G. Roger Jarjoura. 1988. "Social Structure and Criminal Victimization." *Journal of Research in Crime and Delin-quency* 25 (February): 27–52.

Sobran, Joseph. 1997. "FDR Turned Blind Eye to 'Democide' in Soviet Union." *The State*, May 23, A13.

Socolar, Rebecca S., Lisa Amaya-Jackson, Leonard D. Eron, Barbara Howard, John Landsverk, and Jeffery Evans. 1997. "Research on Discipline: The State of the Art, Deficits, and Implications." *Archives of Pediatrics & Adolescent Medicine* 151 (August): 758–60.

Stannard, David E. 1992. "Genocide in The Americas." *The Nation* 255 (October 19): 430–4.

The State. 1994a. "Man Who Shot Cheating Wife Gets 18-Month Prison Term." October 19, A3.

—— 1994b. "Today It's Cigarettes. Tomorrow?" November 1, B5.

—— 1994c. "Court Rules Drunkenness is Defense." November 16, A4.

—— 1994d. "Israeli Court Decision Recognizes Gay Couples." De-cember 1, A4.

—— 1995. "Troublemaker List Divides Georgia Town." February 2, A3.

—— 1996a. "U.N. Says 45 Million Abortions Performed Per Year in World." February 15, A4.

—— 1996b. "School Board Bans All Clubs to Quash Gay Organization." February 22, A3.

—— 1996c. "Cambodians Cooperate in Cheating." July 4, A4.

——1996d. "Modesty Squads Spark Clashes in Jerusalem." August 5, A4.

—— 1996e. "NASCAR Fines Crew Chiefs." August 13, C3.

—— 1996f. "Teen Drug Use Soaring, Survey Finds." August 21, A1, A6.

—— 1997a. "Beggar Youths an Export for India." January 21, A5.

—— 1997b. "Mississippi Bans Same-Sex Marriages." February 13, A3.

—— 1997c. "Tokyo Prostitutes Focus of 'Lolita Complex.'" April 6, A8.

—— 1997d. "Study Records Decline in Crime." April 14, A3.

—— 1997e. "Study Claims Mandatory Sentences Ineffective." May 13, A7.

Steffensmeier, Darrell J., and Robert M. Terry. 1973. "Deviance and Respectability: An Observational Study of Reactions to Shoplifting." *Social Forces* 51 (June): 417–26.

Steinberg, Laurence, with B. Bradford Brown and Sanford M. Dornbusch. 1996. *Beyond the Classroom: Why School Reform Has Failed and What Parents Need to Do*. New York: Simon and Schuster.

Stewart, Robert L. Forthcoming. *Living and Acting Together*. Dix Hills, N.Y.: General Hall.

Straus, Murray A. 1991. "Discipline and Deviance: Physical Punishment of Children and Violence and Other Crime in Adulthood." *Social Problems* 38 (May): 133–54.

Straus, Murray A., with Denise A. Donnelly. 1994. *Beating the Devil Out of Them: Corporal Punishment in American Families*. New York: Lexington Books.

Straus, Murray A., and Richard J. Gelles. 1988. "How Violent Are American Families? Estimates from the National Family Violence Resurvey and Other Studies." Pp. 14–35 in *Family Abuse and Its Consequences: New Directions in Research*, ed. G. Hotaling, D. Finkelhor, J. Kirkpatrick, and M. Straus. Newbury Park, Calif: Sage.

Straus, Murray A., David B. Sugarman, and Jean Giles-Sims. 1997. "Spanking by Parents and Subsequent Antisocial Behavior of Children." *Archives of Pediatrics & Adolescent Medicine* 151 (August): 761–7.

Sykes, Gresham M., and David Matza. 1957. "Techniques of Neutralization: A Theory of Delinquency." *American Sociological Review* 42 (December): 664–70.

Tittle, Charles R. 1980. *Sanctions and Social Deviance*: *The Question of Detererrence*. New York: Praeger.

Tittle, Charles R., Wayne J. Villemez, and Douglas A. Smith. 1978. "The Myth of Social Class and Criminality: An Empirical Assessment of the Empirical Evidence." *American Sociological Review* 43 (October): 643–56.

U.S. Bureau of the Census. 1996. *Statistical Abstract of the United States*: *1996*. 116th ed. Washington, D.C.: Government Printing Office.

U.S. Sentencing Commission. 1995a. *Cocaine and Federal Sentencing Policy*. Washington, D.C.: Government Printing Office.

—— 1995b. *Guidelines Manual*, §3E1.1. November.

Vartabedian, Ralph. 1996. "To File or Not to File? 6 Million Don't." *The State*, April 14, A1, A11.

Wallerstein, James S., and Clement J. Wyle. 1947. "Our Law-abiding Law-breakers." *Probation* 25: 107–112.

Warren, Wendy, and Clif LeBlanc. 1995. "Union Neighbors Couldn't Condemn 'Disturbed' Mom to Electric Chair." *The State*, July 29, A1, A9.

Wechsler, Henry, Andrea Davenport, George Dowdall, Barbara Moeykens, and Sonia Castillo. 1994. "Health and Behavioral Consequences of Binge Drinking in College." *Journal of the American Medical Association* 272 (December 7): 1672–77.

Wilbanks, William. 1987. *The Myth of a Racist Criminal Justice System*. Monterey, Calif.: Brooks/Cole.

Wilkerson, Karen. 1974. "The Broken Family and Juvenile Delinquency: Scientific Explanation or Ideology?" *Social Problems* 21 (June): 726–39.

Wilson, James Q., and Richard J. Herrnstein. 1985. *Crime and Human Nature*. New York: Simon and Schuster.

Wilson, William Julius. 1996. *When Work Disappears*: *The World of the New Urban Poor*. New York: Knopf.

Wiseman, Jacqueline P. 1970. *Stations of the Lost*: *The Treatment of Skid Row Alcoholics*. Englewood Cliffs, N.J.: Prentice Hall.

Zupan, Fran H. 1994. "Mother Pleads Guilty to Neglect in Girl's Death." *The State*, June 10, A1, A6.

ABOUT THE AUTHOR

Paul Higgins grew up in a family of five children outside of Washinton, D.C. His parents, both deaf, taught at Gallaudet University, a university that primarily educates deaf adults. Before attending graduate school in sociology at Northwestern University, where he earned his Ph.D., he taught one year at a state school in Maine that educates deaf children. He now lives in Columbia, South Carolina, with his wife Leigh and their two daughters, Samantha and Cole. He teaches, researches and writes about social life at the University of South Carolina. Among his works are *Outsiders in a Hearing World, The Rehabilitation Detectives, Making Disability, Sociological Wonderment,* and *Understanding Deviance* (with Richard Butler).

INDEX